God's
Wake-Up
Call

Ervin N. Hershberger

Vision Publishers, Inc.
Harrisonburg, Virginia

Published by Vision Publishers, Inc.
Harrisonburg, Virginia

Cover design: Lonnie D. Yoder

For additional copies or comments write to:
Vision Publishers, Inc.
P.O. Box 190
Harrisonburg, VA 22803
Fax: 540-432-6530
e-mail: visionpubl@ntelos.net
(see order form in back)

Table of Contents

Publisher's Note 5

Introduction 8

Preface 10

1   Beware of False Prophets 15

2   Beware of Covetousness 25

3   Beware of Neglect 33

4   Beware of Unbelief 44

5   Beware of Falling Away 59

6   Beware of Sinning Willfully 68

7   Beware of Drawing Back 79

8   Beware of Not Hearing
     Jesus Christ 90

9   Beware of Satan's Trinity 107

10   Be Aware of God's
     Holy Trinity 118

Publisher's Note

"My bags are packed, I am ready to go." These were the words of Ervin N. Hershberger when he was asked how he was. This man of God, knowing that his earthly sojourn was drawing to a close, had made "his calling and election sure." Because of his careful walk of faith in the finished work of Jesus Christ, he was unafraid to die; in fact, he spoke freely of departing this life to be with the Lord. The three lonely years after his wife Barbara's death made him long for heaven even more.

He was a man of prayer. Rising early while many slept, he spent daily time alone with the Lord in prayer, mentioning those of his congregation by name, both young and old alike. It was no wonder that there was a power that worked in this man's life and in others with whom he labored.

Brother Ervin was largely self-educated and a diligent student of the Scriptures. This is reflected in his amazing insights into the "hidden" truths of God's Word.

His special interest was the Tabernacle and the Old Testament. Of particular joy to him was discovering Christ foreshadowed and foretold in many less obvious places. The books he wrote were largely the culmination of the many years he spent in these studies. His first two books show Christ reflected in the Tabernacle and the Old Testament. His third book shows how God worked through committed human instrumentality in the Old and New Testaments. This, his fourth book, reveals his deep concern that people understand the need to follow God fully.

Upon learning of his death, we were concerned as to what he had done with the manuscript of this book that had been returned to him for review. Unknown to us, he had mailed the manuscript and it arrived the day following his funeral, again reminding us that God is always on time.

Brother Ervin remained active until his death. The day of his death he assisted other members of the congregation with the annual cleaning of the church building. After his evening meal and a short rest, he returned to join the youth group in completing the task. As this 89-year-old (young) saint was pushing the vacuum sweeper in the basement, he fell over and was gone. What a glorious blessing it is for a group of young people to carry such a beautiful memory of servanthood through life!

Brother Ervin is like Abel, of whom the Scripture says in Hebrews 11:4, "he being dead yet speaketh." Faithful saints of God are indeed having a wonderful impact on lives today. Will you, dear reader, allow this book to help make you into a faithful saint that will bless still other's lives?

Introduction

I met Ervin Hershberger late one evening as he welcomed our family into his home for a four-day stay in the summer of 1984. We had traveled to that area for a church meeting and the lodging committee had placed us with Brother Ervin and his dear wife. What an enjoyable time we had as we became acquainted and he led precious devotional times. Our last visit with this dear brother was in the spring of 2003 when he entertained us for an evening meal in his home.

Brother Ervin was a man of the Book. His life reflected the Lord of the Book. He never tired of investigating the deeper meanings of the Word of God. Emanating humility, he led a life of servanthood. A devoted churchman, he adorned the office of Deacon. His passing leaves a void among God's servants laboring here on earth.

God's Wake-Up Call represents a summary of Hershberger's lifetime of study in the book of Hebrews. The applications to the contemporary scene are pertinent and much needed in the church today.

In ten penetrating chapters, the author warns, instructs and admonishes the reader in the "most holy faith." He who earnestly reads is wise.

—Paul M. Emerson

Preface

The Book of Hebrews impresses me as an epistle addressed especially to God's own people,[1] which in the New Testament includes Christians of all nations as well as the seed of Abraham.[2] In this epistle, six major warnings reveal God's heart of love reaching out to reclaim those purchased loved ones who have grown careless, indifferent, lukewarm, or even cold. That observation is what prompted the writing of this booklet.

God's most basic attribute is *holiness*. Holiness is the motivating channel and controlling influence of all His moral attributes. God Himself is holiness personified.[3] His holy love can neither approve nor simply ignore sin, lukewarmness, or indifference. That is why He so lovingly calls us to wake up, pay earnest attention to His written Word (the Bible), and exercise an unshakable faith in Him. God knows all about the past and the future as well as the present, and intensely cares for each one of us.

Although we have been saved by grace, we are always in need of constant cleansing, progressive sanctification, and a growing faith in God. The first two wake-up calls addressed in this book came from the lips of Jesus. Recorded in the Gospels, they are meant for everyone who chooses to be a disciple of Jesus. He lovingly warns us to beware of false prophets, who attack us from without, and covetousness, which springs from within, because He knows how susceptible we are. These are two typical examples of the many evils that attack us from without and from within.

The next six warnings come from the Book of Hebrews, and each addresses a very pertinent danger. Neglect is always common among all who await a more convenient season. Unbelief is the very opposite of faith, and perhaps its greatest enemy. Falling away, sinning willfully, and drawing back are three of the saddest tragedies into which a soul could possibly plunge. Having been enlightened, having had a taste of saving grace, having been almost persuaded, yet lost forever probably is more torturous than heathen darkness where truth was never known.

The last warning in the Book of Hebrews says, "Refuse not him that speaketh . . . [making special mention of] him that speaketh from heaven."[4] Many of the wake-up calls mentioned in this book bear the authority of Jesus Christ Himself. Eight times while here on earth in the flesh, He said, "He that hath ears to hear let him hear."[5] Eight other times He spoke from heaven through the Apostle John, saying, "He that hath an ear to hear, let him hear."[6]

The closing verses of The Revelation warn us not to add to or "take away from the words of the book of this prophesy."[7] Living in a land of Bibles, we have no excuse to be ignorant of what God has said. "For the prophecy came not in old time by the will of man: but holy men of God spake as they were moved by the Holy Ghost."[8] It behooves us to be diligent students of the Bible, which calls us to an unshakable faith in a God who knows and cares.

We need to test our beliefs and doctrines, not by our human reasoning, but by God's inspired Word. We need to examine our views prayerfully, correcting anything that conflicts with Bible prophecies or New Testament doctrine. Every prophecy of Christ's first advent has been fulfilled literally. This should assure us that the prophecies of His second advent also will be fulfilled.

What then shall we do with the scores of prophetic passages throughout the Bible declaring the Messianic reign of Christ? We do not understand them all, but is it not safer to trust God and His Word than to distort the meaning of simple words to make them fit our own ideas? God expects us to believe His Word, trusting Him by faith, even when we do not understand.

The Revelation foretells the rise of Satan's trinity: the *dragon,* the *beast,* and the *false prophet.*[9] Satan can never produce anything similar to God's Trinity, but he will try his hardest to fake the trinity by which unbelievers and many halfhearted professing Christians may be deceived. The Revelation also reveals Satan's final thrust, and the certainty of his eternal doom.

Praise God for making us aware of God's Holy Trinity, the grand climax of all authority, by whom the universe and we have been created. That is the Trinity Whom we can fully trust for our protection and redemption.

Thank God for His wake-up calls today, and for His overruling victory and righteous judgment guaranteed to prevail at the end. "Even so, come, Lord Jesus."[10]

—Ervin N. Hershberger

1. Hebrews 1: 1, 2; 2:1-3; 3:1.
2. Genesis 17:7, 8; Exodus 19:5; Deuteronomy 7:6; 14:2; 26:17-19; 1 Kings 8:53; Psalm 33:12; 135:4; Matthew 19:28; Luke 22:29, 30; Revelation 7:3-8.
3. Isaiah 6:3; Romans 4:16; Revelation 15:4.
4. Hebrews 12:25.
5. Matthew 11:15; 13:9, 43; Mark 4:9, 23; 7:16; Luke 8:8; 14:35.
6. Revelation 2:7, 11, 17, 29; 3:6, 13, 22; 13:9.
7. Revelation 22:18, 19.
8. 2 Peter 1:21.
9. Revelation 13:1, 11; 16:13, 14; 19:20; 20:10.
10. Revelation 22:20b.

1

Beware of False Prophets

> Beware of false prophets, which come to you in sheep's clothing, but inwardly they are ravening wolves (Matthew 7:15).

> Take heed and beware of the leaven of the Pharisees and the Sadducees (Matthew 16:6).

These words, spoken by our loving Savior Jesus Christ, reflect His deep concern for the protection of His followers. He was quite familiar with religious leaders who possessed official credentials yet proved to be false teachers. With heartfelt concern, He most lovingly warns us to beware of them.

> He came unto his own, and his own
> received him not. But as many as
> received him, to them gave he power
> to become the sons of God, even to
> them that believe on his name (John
> 1:11, 12).

It was primarily His own people, sitting "in Moses' seat,"[1] of whom He warned His disciples. The scribes and Pharisees tenaciously clung to the Mosaic law, which neither their fathers nor they "were able to bear,"[2] and totally rejected Christ, who alone is able to keep all who truly trust in Him. They plotted and demanded His crucifixion, then martyred most of His Apostles. Jesus, who experienced the thrust of their apostasy firsthand, sincerely cautions us to beware of their erroneous doctrines.

It takes more than a religious profession, water baptism, and church membership to cleanse us from our own self-life. Only the blood of Christ can deliver us from "the lust of the flesh, and the lust of the eyes, and the pride of life, [which] is not of the Father, but is of the world."[3] "If any man love the world, the love of the Father is not in him."[4] These two loves can neither blend nor mix. They are incompatible.

Today we have in print both the New Testament and the Old Testament. It is our privilege and duty to be familiar with God's written Word so we can discern truth and error, rejecting error and embracing truth. Christless orthodoxy and modern philosophy are equally fatal. We may safely trust and follow only prophets and teachers who are true and faithful to the Word of God.

Whether a prophet teaches works without faith or faith without works, the hearer must beware. Salvation depends on a saving faith in the Lord Jesus Christ, a faith that works. To assume that we can earn or obtain salvation by works is fatal. Good works are as empty of saving power as toy money is of buying power. Salvation is provided through the shed blood of Christ and obtained through the obedience of faith.[5]

> Neither is there salvation in any other: for there is none other name under heaven given among men, whereby we must be saved (Acts 4:12).

> For in Jesus Christ neither circumcision availeth any thing, nor uncircumcision; but faith which worketh by love (Galatians 5:6).

> But . . . faith without works is dead. . . . For as the body without the spirit is dead, so faith without works is dead also (James 2:20, 26).

Works are the fruit of faith but not the means of regeneration. The absence of works proves an absence of faith. When God commanded Abraham to offer Isaac as a burnt offering, Abraham proved his faith by his works. He "believed God, and it [his trusting obedience] was imputed unto him for righteousness." [6]

Hebrews 11, the faith chapter, tells us how Old and New Testament saints alike obtained marvelous blessings from God. Sixteen times it says "by faith," five times "through faith," and twice "by it," meaning faith. Without faith it is impossible to please God or to obtain salvation.

Concerning prophets or teachers, Jesus said,

> By their fruits ye shall know them. Not every one that saith unto me, Lord, Lord, shall enter into the kingdom of heaven; but he that doeth the will of my Father which is in heaven (Matthew 7:20, 21).

The will of God is revealed to us through the Word of God, by which all prophets and teachers must be tested.

Through the writings of His Apostles, Jesus continues His warning that we should beware of false prophets and teachers.

> But there were false prophets also among the people, even as there shall be false teachers among you, who privily shall bring in damnable heresies, even denying the Lord that bought them, and bring upon themselves swift destruction. And many shall follow their pernicious ways; by reason of

whom the way of truth shall be evil spoken of. And through covetousness shall they with feigned words make merchandise of you: whose judgment now of a long time lingereth not, and their damnation slumbereth not (2 Peter 2:1-3).

God knows how much we need to beware of false prophets manipulating their way into our hearts. Not all prophets and religious teachers are living in Christ.

For such are false apostles, deceitful workers, transforming themselves into the apostles of Christ. And no marvel; for Satan himself is transformed into an angel of light. Therefore it is no great thing if his ministers also be transformed as the ministers of righteousness; whose end shall be according to their works (2 Corinthians 11:13-15).

Deceitful workers were busy when Christ was here in the flesh. They continued in the days of Paul, and we have them among us today. The major difference is that today mass media multiplies their influence a thousand-fold. Gullible sign seekers are ready prey for Satan's wonder workers, whose heyday may be just around the corner. To the Apostle John, it was revealed that the worst is yet to come, and that it is coming speedily!

> And I beheld another beast coming up out of the earth; and he had two horns like a lamb, and he spake as a dragon. And he exerciseth all the power of the first beast before him, and causeth the earth and them which dwell therein to worship the first beast, whose deadly wound was healed. And he doeth great wonders, so that he maketh fire come down from heaven on the earth in the sight of men, And deceiveth them that dwell on the earth by the means of those miracles which he had power to do in the sight of the beast; saying to them that dwell on the earth, that they should make an image to the beast, which had the wound by a sword, and did live. And he had power to give life unto the image of the beast, that the image of the beast should both speak, and cause that as many as would not

worship the image of the beast should be killed (Revelation 13:11-15).

Some of these things seemed impossible eighty years ago, but God knew it was coming. He chose to use the last survivor of the twelve Apostles to forewarn us nineteen hundred years in advance. Now we can see it on the threshold, leaving us no excuse for ignorance. By reading our Bible, we hear God's trumpet sounding the alarm.

> Then whosoever heareth the sound of the trumpet, and taketh not warning; if the sword come, and take him away, his blood shall be upon his own head. He heard the sound of the trumpet, and took not warning; his blood shall be upon him. But he that taketh warning shall deliver his soul (Ezekiel 33:4, 5).

With false religious teachings, people confront us publicly and privately through books, advertisements, pictures, voices, billboards, magazines, videos, radio, television, and other modern technology. God knows better than we do that many deceptive voices are afloat on the air waves and on the internet. The more we expose ourselves to them, the more we intensify the danger. Will-power often falls prey to curiosity, and "sin lieth at the door."[7] Many a Cain, before he realizes what is happening, finds himself departing "from the presence of the LORD"[8] and caught in a trap he had committed himself to avoid.

The only way to victory is to cast ourselves unreservedly into the embrace of Him who pleads invitingly, "I am the way, the truth, and the life: no man cometh unto the Father, but by me."[9]

Beware of false prophets. They may be highly skilled and extremely persuasive. But it is the undergirding of supernatural forces that makes them as deceptive as the underworld can make them. Human wit and wisdom are ready tools of subversive powers. Only in Christ, kept by the Holy Spirit, can man be delivered from Satan's final thrust. It was of endtime events that Jesus said, "Take heed that no man deceive you."[10]

1. Matthew 23:2.
2. Acts 15:10.
3. 1 John 2:16.
4. 1 John 2:15.
5. Romans 1:5; 16:26b.
6. James 2:23.
7. Genesis 4:7b.
8. Genesis 4:16a.
9. John 14:6.
10. Matthew 24:4.

2

Beware of Covetousness

> Take heed, and beware of covetousness: for a man's life consisteth not in the abundance of the things which he possesseth (Luke 12:15).

In chapter one we looked at Jesus' warning that we should beware of false prophets. In this chapter we examine our own hearts and beware of the evils Jesus described as springing up from within us.

> For from within, out of the heart of men, proceed evil thoughts, adulteries, fornications, murders, thefts, covetousness, wickedness, deceit, lasciviousness, an evil eye, blasphemy, pride, foolishness: all these evil things come

from within, and defile the man (Mark 7:21-23).

The thirteen evils listed all spring "out of the heart of men."[1] Jesus, as God the Son, was confirming what God the Father had said in the days of Noah:

> And God saw that the wickedness of man was great in the earth, and that every imagination of the thoughts of his heart was only evil continually (Genesis 6:5).

> For the imagination of man's heart is evil from his youth (Genesis 8:21b).

> The heart is deceitful above all things, and desperately wicked: who can know it? (Jeremiah 17:9).

The basic problem is our unregenerate nature, with its natural tendency toward the subversive powers of greed. We need the grace of God to discern properly between right and wrong, and especially to reject and to flee from everything that is not for the glory of God.

Covetousness is listed among the vilest of sins, as an evil that must be put to death.

> Mortify [put to death] therefore . . . fornication, uncleanness, inordinate affection, evil concupiscence, and covetousness, which is idolatry: for which things' sake the wrath of God cometh on the children of disobedience (Colossians 3:5, 6).

> For the love of money is the root of all evil (1 Timothy 6:10).

Covetousness has a subtle way of competing with Christ for priority. We seem to have an inborn craving for more than our share of whatever we desire, and even for things that rightly belong to someone else. We can covet money, position, promotion, honor, fame, popularity, praise, and anything else that a human ego could desire. Covetousness is a tragic craving that seldom is fully satisfied. Its antonyms, "liberality," "benevolence," and "generosity," produce far more happiness at every level than covetousness does at any level.

Covetousness is named in Paul's list of twenty-two sins, of which he concludes that they which commit such things are worthy of death.[2] He says the downward plunge began "because that, when they knew God, they glorified him not as God, neither were thankful."[3] What a tragic end to the path of ingratitude!

We all know that covetousness is sin. It is a miserable attribute by which to live and a tragic condition in which to die. Yet, have you ever heard of a church disciplining a member for covetousness? How often have you heard anyone confess it as a personal sin? This does not mean there are no covetous church members. The fact that Jesus felt the need to warn us suggests otherwise. Perhaps it indicates that covetousness is so deeply hidden in the secret chambers of the heart that it is hard to identify—and even harder to confess.

Covetousness is a sin that thrives under camouflage. The rich young ruler in Mark 10:17-27 was guilty of it and never suspected his sin until Jesus turned the spotlight on it.

If he did not have it, it surely had him, and it seriously threatened his salvation. In fact, anyone who has not learned the grace of contentment probably is infected already with covetousness.

Unfortunately, covetousness is most common among people who have more of this world's goods than they need or can use wisely. We have heard wealthy people boast that they neither lend nor borrow. They glory in their independence, unaware that the sin of covetousness may be the determining factor in their choice of such independence.

The basic secret of survival among poverty-stricken people is sharing with one another. Poverty motivated the Macedonian churches to give liberally!

> Moreover, brethren, we do you to wit of the grace of God bestowed on the churches of Macedonia; how that in a great trial of affliction, the abundance of their joy and their deep poverty abounded unto the riches of their liberality. For to their power, I bear record, yea, and beyond their power they were

willing of themselves; praying us with much entreaty that we would receive the gift, and take upon us the fellowship of the ministering to the saints [at Jerusalem]. And this they did, not as we hoped, but first gave their own selves to the Lord, and unto us by the will of God (2 Corinthians 8:1-5).

Deep poverty had freed these Macedonian Christians from covetousness. It had cured them of many selfish thoughts, and motivated them to give most liberally. Paul and his companions were not taking offerings for themselves, but for needy Christians at Jerusalem. They were amazed by how the Macedonian churches so willingly gave. "Yea, and beyond their power they were willing,"[4] literally begging Paul and his companions to accept it all. Their own economic struggles had made them very sensitive to the needs of others, causing their liberality to flourish.

In Mark 12:41, 42, Jesus observed many that were rich casting in much; however, the poor widow gave all that she had.

And he [Jesus] called unto him his disciples, and saith unto them, Verily I say
unto you, That this poor widow hath
cast more in, than all they which have
cast into the treasury: for all they did
cast in of their abundance; but she of
her want did cast in all that she had,
even all her living (Mark 12:43, 44).

Men counted the money, but Jesus con-
sidered the motive. The rich gave some of
their surplus, expecting to be admired. The
widow gave "all her living," trusting God as
the source of life and sustenance. Jesus, seeing it from God's perspective, valued her con-
tribution more than the lavish abundance
given by the rich.

One of the most solemn warnings against
the sin of covetousness is the fall of Judas
Iscariot. He was one of Jesus' twelve
Apostles, the one they trusted with the
money they shared in common.[5] His access
to the bag got the best of him, reducing him
to a thief,[6] making him willing to sell his Savior for thirty pieces of silver. Jesus said sadly,
"Woe unto that man by whom the Son of man

is betrayed! It had been good for that man if he had not been born."[7] Eternal loss is a horrible price to pay for temporal gain.

Beware of covetousness!

---

1. Mark 7:21a.
2. Romans 1:29-32.
3. Romans 1:21a.
4. 2 Corinthians 8:3.
5. John 13:29.
6. John 12:4-6.
7. Matthew 26:24.

3

Beware of Neglect

Therefore we ought to give the more earnest heed to the things which we have heard, lest at any time we should let them slip. For if the word spoken by angels was stedfast, and every transgression and disobedience received a just recompense of reward; how shall we escape, if we neglect so great salvation; which at the first began to be spoken by the Lord, and was confirmed unto us by them that heard him; God also bearing them witness, both with signs and wonders, and with divers miracles, and gifts of the Holy Ghost, according to his own will? (Hebrews 2:1-4)

This is the first of six solemn warnings in the book of Hebrews. This warning against neglect begins appropriately with *therefore,* the *wherefore* of which is found in the first chapter of Hebrews. This chapter introduces Christ our Savior, who came to earth to redeem mankind from their fallen condition. To neglect His gracious invitation, letting those precious opportunities slip by, closes the door to salvation.

The Hebrew people to whom this epistle was addressed gloried in Abraham, Moses, and the prophets. The writer to the Hebrews needed to convince them that these great men in whom they trusted were God's messengers pointing them to Jesus Christ as the only means unto salvation.

"Abraham believed God, and it [his faith] was counted unto him for righteousness."[1] Moses plainly taught,

> The LORD thy God will raise up unto thee a Prophet [namely, Jesus Christ] from the midst of thee, of thy brethren, like unto me; unto him ye shall hearken (Deuteronomy 18:15).

These men of God were made great by their unwavering faith in the coming Messiah. "And beginning at Moses and all the prophets, he [Jesus] expounded unto them in all the Scriptures the things concerning himself."[2]

> God, who at sundry times and in divers manners spake in time past unto the fathers by the prophets, hath in these last days spoken unto us by his Son, whom he hath appointed heir of all things, by whom also he made the worlds; who being the brightness of his glory, and the express image of his person, and upholding all things by the word of his power, when he had by himself purged our sins, sat down on the right hand of the Majesty on high (Hebrews 1:1-3).

These three verses name eight things that make Christ superior to all others:

- He is God's Son.
- He is heir of all things.
- He made the worlds.

- He is the brightness of God's glory.
- He is the express image of God.
- He upholds all things by His powerful Word.
- He purged our sins.
- He sat down on the right hand of God.

Besides the Holy Trinity, not one being in heaven or on earth can claim any one of these eight superlatives.

The writer continues, showing that Jesus not only surpasses great men on earth, but that He also is superior to the greatest and most holy angels of heaven.

> Being made so much better than the angels, as he hath by inheritance obtained a more excellent name than they. For unto which of the angels said he at any time, Thou art my Son, this day have I begotten thee? And again, I will be to him a Father, and he shall be to me a Son? And again, when he bringeth in the firstbegotten into the world, he saith, And let all the angels of God worship him (Hebrews 1:4-6).

True worship is directed strictly to Deity.

"Thou shalt worship the Lord thy God, and him only shalt thou serve."[3] The title "Lord God" obviously includes the Lord Jesus Christ.

> Therefore let all the house of Israel know assuredly, that God hath made that same Jesus, whom ye have crucified, both Lord and Christ (Acts 2:36).

And God had commanded all the holy angels to worship that same Jesus.[4] His deity is most thoroughly confirmed throughout the Word of God.[5]

These are the foundational truths to which "we ought to give the more earnest heed, . . . lest at any time we should let them slip."[6] That foundation will not slip, but to let go of these basic facts is to slip from the foundation. The writer of Hebrews was deeply concerned for the salvation of his own people. He knew the fatality of not knowing Jesus.[7] All through chapter one he continues, finally quoting from the Psalms to prove that the Hebrew psalmists recognized the promised Christ as preeminent over all men and all angels.

7. And of the angels he saith, Who maketh his angels spirits, and his ministers a flame of fire. **8.** But unto the Son he saith, Thy throne, O God, is for ever and ever: a sceptre of righteousness is the sceptre of thy kingdom. **9.** Thou hast loved righteousness, and hated iniquity; therefore God, even thy God, hath anointed thee with the oil of gladness above thy fellows. **10.** And, Thou, Lord, in the beginning hast laid the foundation of the earth; and the heavens are the works of thine hands: **11.** They shall perish; but thou remainest; and they all shall wax old as doth a garment; **12.** And as a vesture shalt thou fold them up, and they shall be changed: but thou art the same, and thy years shall not fail. **13.** But to which of the angels said he at any time, Sit on my right hand, until I make thine enemies thy footstool? **14.** Are they not all ministering spirits, sent forth to minister for them who shall be heirs of salvation? (Hebrews 1:7-14).

You will find that verses 8 and 9 quote

Psalm 45:6, 7, and that verses 10 to 12 quote
Psalm 102:25-27. The word "and" at the beginning of verse 10 links the second passage
to the beginning of verse 8, affirming that
both passages had been said "unto the Son."
The latter part of verse 12 is applied specifi-
cally to Jesus in Hebrews 13:8. Hebrews 1:13
is a repeat of Psalm 110:1, and the roots for
verse 14 spring from Psalm 103:20, 21.

The Psalms, written by Hebrew writers,
were used as the nation's hymnal. Many
people, however, failed to grasp the prophetic praises of Christ's future glory that the
Psalms plainly foretold. God provided the
Epistle to the Hebrews to convince unbelieving Jews that David and other psalmists
whom they admired actually had proclaimed
Christ long before He came in the flesh.

God, in His goodness, has provided perfect and full salvation for all who by faith
receive Christ, and who abide in Him to the
end.[8]

> Behold therefore the goodness and se-
> verity of God: on them which fell, se-
> verity; but toward thee, goodness, if

thou continue in his goodness: otherwise thou also shalt be cut off (Romans 11:22).

To neglect so great a salvation leads to a tragedy from which there is no escape.

Neglect, according to *Strong's Concordance*, means "to be careless of: make light of." Neglect can happen without effort, without thinking, and without our notice. Satan, the master deceiver, delights to keep our mind occupied with the cares and pleasures of this world. He cares not whether it be something good or bad, as long as it distracts us from focusing on things eternal. God, who made us for eternity, has carefully planned a great salvation that we cannot afford to neglect.

Salvation definitely requires a divine Savior! Every human stain must be washed clean by the sinless blood of Christ. The blood that Christ shed for us on Calvary is sufficient to save the worst of sinners who lay hold on Him by simple, trusting faith. "But without faith it is impossible to please him,"[9] or to obtain salvation by any other means. Neither Noah, Job, Abraham, Moses, Daniel, nor any other person ever was or ever will be saved except by faith in that great salvation through the blood of Christ.[10]

Redemption is God's work of grace through our Savior Jesus Christ, and "we have access by faith into this grace."[11] We are purified by faith, sanctified by faith, justified by faith, stand by faith, walk by faith, and shall live by faith.[12] In fact, "the scripture hath concluded all under sin, that the promise by faith of Jesus Christ might be given to them that believe."[13]

Salvation is profoundly simple yet simply profound! It is not an accomplishment that the most able might attain by self-effort, but a gift of grace that anyone may obtain by a simple, sincere, childlike faith in Christ. Yet the vast majority plunge to eternal doom simply because they neglect, ignore, or esteem lightly the great salvation that God so freely offers. When such neglect continues until death, there is no escape.

To faithful believers the promise remains:

As we have borne the image of the earthy, we shall also bear the image of the heavenly (1 Corinthians 15:49).

Behold, I show you a mystery; We shall not all sleep, but we shall all be changed, in a moment, in the twinkling of an eye, at the last trump: for the trumpet shall sound, and the dead shall be raised incorruptible, and we shall be changed. For this corruptible must put on incorruption, and this mortal must put on immortality. So when this corruptible shall have put on incorruption, and this mortal shall have put on immortality, then shall be brought to pass the saying that is written, Death is swallowed up in victory. O death, where *is* thy sting? O grave, where *is* thy victory? (1 Corinthians 15:51-55).

But thanks be to God, which giveth us the victory through our Lord Jesus Christ. Therefore, my beloved brethren, be ye steadfast, unmovable, always abounding in the work of the Lord, forasmuch as ye know that your labour is not in vain in the Lord (1 Corinthians 15:57, 58).

Beware of neglect. Tomorrow may be too late.

---

1. Romans 4:3; Galatians 3:6; James 2:23.
2. Luke 24:27.
3. Matthew 4:10b; Luke 4:8b.
4. Hebrews 1:6.
5. Philippians 2:9-11.
6. Hebrews 2:1.
7. Acts 9:1-5.
8. John 15:2-7.
9. Hebrews 11:6.
10. Acts 4:12.
11. Romans 5:2.
12. Acts 15:9; 26:18; Romans 3:28; 11:20; 2 Corinthians 1:24; 5:7; Galatians 3:11.
13. Galatians 3:22.

4

Beware of Unbelief

Take heed, brethren, lest there be in any of you an evil heart of unbelief, in departing from the living God (Hebrews 3:12).

O LORD, I know that the way of man is not in himself: it is not in man that walketh to direct his steps (Jeremiah 10:23).

Therefore, we must put our faith and trust in the Lord Jesus Christ, who came from heaven to be our Savior and our Guide.

The Background

The warning in Hebrews 3:7–4:1, the sec-

ond and longest in the book of Hebrews,
is based on a happening in Israel's his-
tory. The children of Israel had seen God
demonstrate His mighty power in the ten
plagues of Egypt. He had parted the Red
Sea by stacking up the water like walls
on each side and bringing Israel through
on dry ground. Then He had brought the
waters crashing down, drowning the
Egyptian army and their horses.[1]

The bitter waters of Marah He had
made sweet with a tree, so the Israelites
could drink.[2] One evening He had covered their camp with quail for supper,
and in the morning He had rained bread
from heaven.[3] Then, all through their wilderness journey, He had fed them daily
with manna. He had brought a river of
water out of the smitten rock in Horeb,
and had delivered them from the armies
of Amalek.[4] God had brought them safely
through "that great and terrible wilderness, wherein were fiery serpents, and
scorpions, and drought."[5] To every problem they encountered, He had been the

perfect, never-failing solution.[6]

All this, and much more, they had witnessed and experienced. God had brought them to the very borders of Canaan, and had promised,

> I will send an angel before thee; and I will drive out the Canaanite, the Amorite, and the Hittite, and the Perizzite, the Hivite, and the Jebusite (Exodus 33:2).

Yet, they did not trust God to do what He had promised. Hear Moses tell the story.

> And I said unto you, Ye are come unto the mountain of the Amorites, which the LORD our God doth give unto us. Behold, the LORD thy God hath set the land before thee: go up and possess it, as the LORD God of thy fathers hath said unto thee; fear not, neither be discouraged. And ye came near unto me every one of you, and said, We will send men before us, and they shall search us out the land, and bring us word again by what way we must go up, and into what cities we shall come. And the say-

ing pleased me well: and I took twelve
men of you, one of a tribe: and they . . .
searched it out (Deuteronomy 1:20-24).

They were more willing to trust the rec-
ommendation of human spies than the omniscience, grace, and promises of Almighty
God. Their suggestion even pleased Moses.
Because of their request, God told Moses to
select one man from each tribe [substituting
the tribes of Ephraim and Manasseh for the
tribes of Levi and Joseph].[7] Ten of the twelve
spies were more impressed with the giants
than with the promises and power of God.
Believing the spies more than they believed
God, the people rebelled against the commandment of the Lord. And God said,

Because all those men which have seen
my glory, and my miracles, which I did
in Egypt and in the wilderness, and
have tempted me now these ten times,
and have not hearkened to my voice;
surely they shall not see the land which
I sware unto their fathers, neither shall
any of them that provoked me see it
(Numbers 14:22, 23).

For the complete story, study Numbers 13:26–14:15.   Here again the Israelites had said, "Would God that we had died in the land of Egypt! Or would God we had died in this wilderness!" Therefore God took them up on their request and said,

> Your carcasses shall fall in this wilderness; and all that were numbered of you, according to your whole number, from twenty years old and upward, which have murmured against me, doubtless ye shall not come into the land, concerning which I sware to make you dwell therein, save Caleb the son of Jephunneh, and Joshua the son of Nun. But your little ones, which ye said should be a prey, them will I bring in, and they shall know the land which ye have despised. But as for you, your carcasses, they shall fall in this wilderness. And your children shall wander in the wilderness forty years, and bear your whoredoms, until your carcasses be wasted in the wilderness (Numbers 14:29-33).

Because of their unbelief and rebellion, they had to wander another thirty-eight years in the wilderness, until all the men of war, except Caleb and Joshua, had died. That disaster is the background of this most lengthy warning in the book of Hebrews.

The Warning

The warning may be divided into four paragraphs. The roots of the first paragraph are found in Psalm 95:7b-11, which Hebrews 4:7 credits to David:

> Wherefore as the Holy Ghost saith, Today if ye will hear his voice, harden not your hearts, as in the provocation, in the day of temptation in the wilderness: When your fathers tempted me, proved me, and saw my works forty years. Wherefore I was grieved with that generation, and said, They do alway err in their heart; and they have not known my ways. So I sware in my wrath, They shall not enter into my rest. (Hebrews 3:7-11).

The second paragraph, addressing New Testament and church age situations, is especially pertinent for us today. It diagnoses the tendency of man to do evil, explaining the hardening effects and deceitfulness of sin. But it also assures us that in Christ there is power for Christians to overcome.

> Take heed, brethren, lest there be in any of you an evil heart of unbelief, in departing from the living God. But exhort one another daily, while it is called Today; lest any of you be hardened through the deceitfulness of sin. For we are made partakers of Christ, if we hold the beginning of our confidence steadfast unto the end; while it is said, Today if ye will hear his voice, harden not your hearts, as in the provocation [at Kadesh-barnea, Deuteronomy 1:19-22] (Hebrews 3:12-15).

In the third paragraph, the writer of Hebrews grieves for the estimated one and one-half million souls (including 603,550 men of war, their wives, and in some cases their children) who perished in the wilderness through unbelief. Although the word "unbelief" is not found in the KJV Old Testament, the malignancy of it has been very much in evidence ever since the fall of man. It is no wonder that the writer to the Hebrews feared for the unbelieving Jews of his day, and for the wayward defectors of our day.

> For some, when they had heard, did provoke: howbeit not all that came out of Egypt by Moses. But with whom was he grieved forty years? was it not with them that had sinned, whose carcasses fell in the wilderness? And to whom sware he that they should not enter into his rest, but to them that believed not? So we see that they could not enter in because of unbelief (Hebrews 3:16-19).

In the fourth paragraph, the writer says, "Let us therefore fear, lest, a promise being left us of entering into his rest, any of you should seem to come short of it."[8] This verse is tailor-made for modern day Christians who after lifelong opportunities to benefit from all these Biblical records, still seem to come short of victories they should and could be experiencing in Christ.

The Problem

In some sin-darkened countries today, the Gospel light is beginning to dawn, and churches are growing rapidly. But "enlightened" North Americans seem to be gospel hardened, and churches are dying. God measures spiritual life neither by enrollment nor activity, but by our commitment and receptivity to His Holy Word and will. Many professing Christians are engulfed in entertainment, the pursuit of pleasure, and the lusts of the flesh.

Every year one and one-half million unborn American babies are sacrificed to the gods of self-indulgence and irresponsibility (misnamed "freedom of choice") with governmental protection and even financial support. Sins thoroughly denounced in both the Old and New Testaments, that our civil laws once prohibited, now are legalized by law and tolerated by many churches.

According to veteran pollster George

Gallup,[9] the lifestyles of many church members have decayed to the levels of general society. Society is not becoming more Christlike, but churchianity is embracing more and more immorality, divorce, remarriage, dishonesty, lying, cheating, pilferage, and the like. God and His Word have not changed and will not change, but churches in unbelief are rapidly ripening for judgment.

Plain (conservative-minded) churches may be relatively free from some of these open and obvious sins, but let us not forget that plain worldliness also is condemned by a just and holy God. Materialism, the love of money, self-centeredness, high-minded thoughts about ourselves, unholy thoughts, and fantasies all are sins that may be hidden from public knowledge, and even from our own personal realization, but not from God, who condemns them.

We may even be guilty of unbelief by unwittingly denying plainly stated prophetic Scriptures. I have been guilty and needed to repent of that myself. God lovingly warns us to beware of unbelief. Let us beware of unwitting oversights that may be unbelief in God's sight.

The Solution

What we need is a living and active faith in a living and active Savior. A dead faith saves no one, but a living faith will save sinners. A living Savior can transform the vilest sinner into a clean, radiant, and victorious Christian. Jesus transformed Saul the persecutor into a dynamic apostle to the Gentiles with a never-dying zeal for his own people as well.

The word *faith,* which occurs only twice in the King James Version of the Old Testament,[10] appears two hundred forty-five times in the New Testament. Paul was a most prolific proponent of faith. *Faith* occurs forty-nine times in Romans, thirty-two times in Hebrews, twenty-two times in Galatians, nineteen times in 1 Timothy, and fifty-nine times in Paul's other epistles (a total of one hundred seventy-one times).

Paul in sincerity, and yet in blind unbelief and error, had devoted himself to persecuting Christians. But after his conversion, and with Jesus reigning in his heart, the flame of faith was never again extinguished in his life. Let Paul tell you what he willingly suffered for the faith that saved his soul.

> Of the Jews five times received I forty stripes save one. Thrice was I beaten with rods, once was I stoned, thrice I suffered shipwreck, a night and a day I have been in the deep; in journeyings often, in perils of waters, in perils of robbers, in perils by mine own countrymen, in perils by the heathen, in perils in the city, in perils in the wilderness, in perils in the sea, in perils among false brethren; in weariness and painfulness, in watchings often, in hunger and thirst, in fastings often, in cold and nakedness (2 Corinthians 11:24-27).

Hebrews 11, the faith chapter, in the first thirty-four verses names sixteen Old Testament heroes, telling of wonders they wrought by faith. It continues with others too numerous to name,

Who through faith subdued kingdoms, wrought righteousness, obtained promises, stopped the mouths of lions, quenched the violence of fire, escaped the edge of the sword, out of weakness were made strong, waxed valiant in fight, turned to flight the armies of the aliens. Women received their dead raised to life again: and others were tortured, not accepting deliverance; that they might obtain a better resurrection: and others had trial of cruel mockings and scourgings, yea, moreover of bonds and imprisonment: they were stoned, they were sawn asunder, were tempted, were slain with the sword: they wandered about in sheepskins and goatskins; being destitute, afflicted, tormented; of whom the world was not worthy: they wandered in deserts, and in mountains, and in dens and caves of the earth. And these all, having obtained a good report through faith, received not the promise: God having provided some better thing for us, that they without us should not be made perfect (Hebrews 11:33-40).

The "better thing" that we now have is the New Testament, the written Gospel of Christ. "For it is the power of God unto salvation to every one that believeth; to the Jew first, and also to the Greek."[11]

> For what the law could not do, in that it was weak through the flesh, God sending his own Son in the likeness of sinful flesh, and for sin, condemned sin in the flesh: that the righteousness of the law might be fulfilled [by Jesus Christ] in us, who walk not after the flesh, but after the Spirit (Romans 8:3, 4).

"Faith is the substance of things hoped for, the evidence of things not seen."[12] Old Testament saints who by faith embraced the promises of God without wavering enjoyed the saving power of God, even though they died as martyrs. Although they "received not the promise" by seeing its fulfillment in this life, they were sealed and safe by faith in the promise, long before Jesus came in the flesh to make that promise good. But we, with the Gospel at hand and all these examples before us, are even more responsible and more accountable than they were.

> For unto whomsoever much is given, of him shall be much required: and to whom men have committed much, of him they will ask the more (Luke 12:48b).

Beware of unbelief!

---

1. Exodus 7:19–15:13.
2. Numbers 15:22-25.
3. Exodus 16:11-15.
4. Exodus 17.
5. Deuteronomy 8:15.
6. Exodus 15:23–17:16.
7. Numbers 13:1-16.
8. Hebrews 4:1.
9. Reported in 1997.
10. Deuteronomy 32:20; Habakkuk 2:4.
11. Romans 1:16.
12. Hebrews 11:1.

5

Beware of Falling Away

For it is impossible for those who were once enlightened, and have tasted of the heavenly gift, and were made partakers of the Holy Ghost, and have tasted the good word of God, and [tasted] the powers of the world to come, if they shall fall away, to renew them again unto repentance; seeing they crucify to themselves the Son of God afresh, and put him to an open shame (Hebrews 6:4-6).

Notice that the text speaks of those who were once enlightened, who had experienced the heavenly gift [divine grace], who had been partakers of the Holy Spirit, who had tasted the good Word of God, and who had [tasted] the powers of the world to come. Can anyone who is not in Christ be a partaker of the Holy Spirit? At least they were more responsible and more accountable than those with fewer opportunities. That much seems reasonably clear. But the falling away and the impossibility of renewing them to repentance calls for serious study with prayer and fasting, lest we misinterpret God's Holy Word.

Some (holding the Calvinistic view) raise questions about the word "if" (if they fall away). To them, the passage presents a hypothetical case. They say it is impossible for any born again believer ever to fall away and be lost. Would God and the Holy Spirit have invested sixty-nine words to warn us about a danger that could never exist? To me, the text seems to warn us about the danger of something that can and does happen, through neglect, unbelief, rebellion, or deliberate and willful violation of better knowledge. Luther's German version does not say "if," but "where."

According to Adam Clarke, the Greek participles in verses 4 and 5 are properly rendered in the past tense: *were enlightened, have tasted,* and *were made partakers.* Therefore he thinks verse 6, instead of saying "if," should say, "have fallen away." I have at least seven other English versions in which that clause is translated in the past tense.

Clarke concludes,

> It appears from this [Hebrews 6:4-8], whatever sentiment may gain or lose by it, that there is a fearful possibility of falling away from the grace of God; and if this Scripture did not say so, there are many that do say so. And were there no Scripture express on this subject, the nature of the present state of man, which is a state of probation or trial, must necessarily imply it. Let him who most assuredly standeth, take heed lest he fall.[1]

We believe that security in Christ is conditional upon our willingness to abide in Him. It is certainly true, as Jesus said, that "no man is able to pluck them out of my Father's hand."[2] It is also true that man is created as a creature of choice, which makes us responsible to choose truth, grace, direction, and God's protection. "Therefore choose life."[3] We must receive Christ by choice, and we must abide in Him by choice according to John 15:1-5. God will not hold us in His hand by force without our consent. Jesus said,

> If a man abide not in me, he is cast forth as a branch, and is withered; and men gather them, and cast them into the fire, and they are burned (John 15:6).

Chapter eight of Romans was written to "the children of God."[4] In it we find at least thirty-two blessings provided for the Christian. In that same chapter, Paul says,

> Therefore, brethren, we are debtors, not to the flesh, to live after the flesh. For if ye live after the flesh, ye shall die: but if ye through the Spirit do mortify the deeds of the body, ye shall live (Romans 8:12, 13).

There we have two "ifs" indicating that the Christian's security is conditional. One is a warning, the other a promise. Is that solemn warning any less certain than the gracious promise? If we deny the certainty of the warning, by what authority can we claim the promise?

You may wonder why it would be impossible to renew them unto repentance. It probably is for the same reason that

> the blasphemy against the Holy Ghost shall not be forgiven unto men. And whosoever speaketh a word against the Son of man, it shall be forgiven him: but whosoever speaketh against the Holy Ghost, it shall not be forgiven him, neither in this world, neither in the world to come (Matthew 12:31b, 32).

Could anyone enlightened and experienced as those described in Hebrews 6:4, 5 fall away without rejecting the wooing of the Holy Spirit?

We may not safely conclude when someone has fallen away beyond the point of no return. I like the little saying (I know not by whom):

> There is a line by us unseen,
> That crosses every path;

The hidden boundary between
God's patience and His wrath.

In His high priestly prayer, Jesus said of
Judas Iscariot, "Those that thou gavest me I
have kept, and none of them is lost, but the
son of perdition."[5] This verse is sometimes
used to prove that Jesus only ever lost one.
That one was among those given to Jesus
while He "was with them in the world."[5] It
does prove that one of them was lost, and
not by any fault, defect, or weakness of Jesus!
It was the result of some choices Judas made
by his own free will.

Judas had been an Apostle of Jesus for
three and one-half years. He had heard a full
course of divine teaching straight from the
lips of Jesus, and had seen the miracles He
performed. I think He heard the warnings at
that last Passover supper when Jesus said,
"Woe unto that man by whom the Son of man
is betrayed! it had been good for that man if
he had not been born."[6] He probably knew
whom Jesus meant when He said, "Ye are
clean, but not all"[7] and "he that eateth bread

with me hath lifted up his heel against me."[8]

Those warning signals must have beckoned Judas to repent of his treacherous plans. He knew right from wrong, but for thirty pieces of silver he chose to do what he knew was wrong. He ignored the tender warnings of Jesus, and chose to proceed with the evil he had planned. The next day he admitted, "I have sinned in that I have betrayed the innocent blood."[9] The guilt gave him no rest, and surely the Holy Spirit pled with him. But Judas stubbornly rejected the Spirit's wooing, "and went and hanged himself."[10] He chose the course that sealed his destiny.

> Among the chief rulers also many believed on [Jesus]; but because of the Pharisees they did not confess him, lest they should be put out of the synagogue: for they loved the praise of men more than the praise of God (John 12:42, 43).

These rulers, too, were choosing destinies. Many were enlightened and convinced, but, like Joseph of Arimathæa, they feared to confess Him. Joseph, however, responded to his convictions when he acquired and buried the crucified body of Jesus.[11] Fear was a very real motivater in those days. Religious persecution abounded. Undoubtedly, many denied Christ just to avoid being expelled from the synagogue. Fearful persecution and the martyrdom of Christians abound today in many countries. The danger of recanting under severe torture is very real!

Paul, before his conversion, persecuted Christians "and compelled them to blaspheme."[12] He realized the possibility of falling because he saw it happen. Therefore, he took warning and kept his body and his carnal nature under, as he said, "lest that by any means, when I have preached unto others, I myself should be a castaway."[13]

Beware of falling away!

1. *Clarke's Commentary*, Volume VI, 1832, page 725.
2. John 10:29.
3. Deuteronomy 30:19.
4. Romans 8:16.
5. John 17:12.
6. Matthew 26:24.
7. John 13:10b.
8. John 13:18.
9. Matthew 27:4.
10. Matthew 27:5.
11. John 19:38.
12. Acts 26:11.
13. 1 Corinthians 9:27.

6

Beware of
Sinning Willfully

> For if we sin willfully after that we
> have received the knowledge of the
> truth, there remaineth no more sacri-
> fice for sins (Hebrews 10:26).

"Willfully" is here translated from
hekousios, a Greek word found only twice in
the KJV Bible. It means "voluntarily," and is
translated "willingly" in 1 Peter 5:2. Luther's
German renders it *mutwillig*, the equivalent
of wanton sport or deliberate malice! It probably is more serious to "sin willfully" than
to be unfaithful under persecution and torture.[1] It implies making light of trusting the

blood of Christ to save us from sin, and includes outright rejection of Jesus as Savior and Lord.

Had not Judas Iscariot "received the knowledge of the truth" during his three years of intimate fellowship with Jesus? Did he not then sin willfully when he voluntarily bargained to betray his Lord and Master for thirty pieces of silver, and then "sought opportunity to betray him"?[2] I believe the preincarnate Christ spoke prophetically, using David as His penman, when he predicted the treachery of Judas, saying, "Yea, mine own familiar friend, in whom I trusted, which did eat of my bread, hath lifted up his heel against me."[3]

Was not the Jewish Sanhedrin deliberately malicious when it sought false witnesses to condemn Jesus to death? Did not the high priests sin willfully when they bribed the soldiers to lie, saying that the disciples stole the body of Jesus while they slept?[4] Were they not deliberately malicious when they denied Peter and John the right to declare the "notable miracle"[5] that no man could deny? They surely had received some knowledge that they violated willfully.

Saul had been "exceedingly mad"[6] in his effort to wipe out Christianity. How were these Christ-hating officials different from Saul before his conversion? I cannot answer that, except with the answers that Paul and Jesus have already given. Paul said, "I have lived in all good conscience before God until this day."[7] "And herein do I exercise myself, to have always a conscience void of offense toward God and toward men."[8] "I thank God, whom I serve from my forefathers with pure conscience."[9] Saul had been absolutely wrong in his early days, but he was honestly and sincerely doing what his authorities had taught him to do. He had not been exposed to the knowledge of the truth as Judas had.

Jesus knew the sincerity of Saul, and what a mighty missionary he would be if he were properly enlightened. He also knew that Judas Iscariot had willingly abandoned a perfect opportunity to be a faithful pillar. So also had the Sanhedrin, and those Jewish officials who against overwhelming evidences, and many perhaps against better knowledge, continued their resistance against Christianity. Jesus clearly understood the difference between Saul and other persecutors long before it was evident to man. Therefore, He chose Saul, the madman, to become Paul the mighty missionary.

Many of those Jewish religious leaders tried desperately to deny the blood atonement and resurrection of Jesus Christ, even against convincing evidences that could neither be concealed nor denied.

For if we sin willfully after that we have received the knowledge of the truth, there remaineth no more sacrifice for sins, but a certain fearful looking for of judgment and fiery indignation, which shall devour the adversaries. He that despised Moses' law died without mercy under two or three witnesses: of how much sorer punishment, suppose ye, shall he be thought worthy, who hath trodden under foot the Son of God, and hath counted the blood of the covenant, wherewith he was sanctified, an unholy thing, and hath done despite unto the Spirit of grace? (Hebrews 10:26-29)

I am afraid many of the described acts had "done despite unto the Spirit of grace." I am inclined to believe that at least some of those who committed these acts must have felt the truth knocking at the door of their heart. But they resisted and fought against knowledge and insight, which the Jewish Scriptures taught abundantly, because "they loved the praise of men more than the praise of God."[10]

What about Ananias and Sapphira, described in Acts 5:1-10? Together they secretly planned a pretense to appear more generous than they really were. There is no indication that Ananias spoke a word when he presented part of the money to the Apostles. He had "not lied unto men, but unto God." Upon hearing Peter's rebuke Ananias dropped dead. Later, not knowing what had happened to Ananias, Sapphira came. Peter asked her if this was the sum of what they received for the land they sold. She answered in the affirmative and also fell down dead.

This reminds us that in the dawn of the Mosaic dispensation, two priests "offered strange fire before the LORD, which he commanded them not. And there went out fire from the LORD, and devoured them."[11] Likewise, at the dawn of Christianity, God gave a similar warning by the death of two people that His abundant grace must be obtained by holy, reverential fear, and humble, sincere obedience to the revealed truth of God.

The Hebrews, to whom this epistle is addressed, are God's "peculiar treasure,"[12] "the apple of his eye."[13] This is one reason why they have been subjected to God's severe discipline. God had said of Israel, "You only have I known of all the families of the earth: therefore I will punish you for all your iniquities."[14] "For whom the Lord loveth he chasteneth, and scourgeth every son whom he receiveth."[15] Because of this and because of their unbelief, the Hebrew people have suffered so often and so intensely for the past two thousand years.

A little story may help us better understand God's special concern and corrective discipline for Israel. Two boys had gotten into a fight in a city park. A man, coming upon the scene, took one of the boys aside and spanked him.

Another observer challenged him, saying, "That's not fair! The other boy was just as bad as this one. Why did you spank one and not the other?"

"Because this one is my son, and the other is not," explained the father.

Notice that this warning against sinning willfully concludes with two partial quotes taken from the writings of Moses in Deuteronomy.

> To me belongeth vengeance, and recompense; their foot shall slide in due time: for the day of their calamity is at hand, and the things that shall come upon them make haste. For the LORD shall judge his people, and repent himself for his servants, when he seeth that their power is gone, and there is none shut up, or left (Deuteronomy 32:35, 36).

For we know him that hath said, Vengeance belongeth unto me, I will recompense, saith the Lord. And again, The Lord shall judge his people (Hebrews 10:30).

Then follows another solemn warning: "It is a fearful thing to fall into the hands of the living God."[16] This may refer to the "fiery indignation" of Hebrews 10:27, probably the fire of hell itself, to which there is no end. But the prophets of Israel spoke extensively of a "great and dreadful day of the Lord"[17] preceding the fire that never ends. The Bible gives that particular time of vengeance and judgment many and various names, of which "the day of the Lord" is the first and by far the most frequent.[18] This speaks of a judgment yet to come, and possibly very soon.

Other possible names for that particular judgment may include the following:
- "the indignation" (Isaiah 26:20; 34:2);
- "the day of the Lord's vengeance" (Isaiah 34:8; 63:1-6);
- "the time of Jacob's trouble" (Jeremiah 30:7);

- "the overspreading of abominations" (Daniel 9:27);
- "the indignation"(Daniel 11:36);
- "a time of trouble, such as never was" (Daniel 12:1);
- "the time of the end" (Daniel 12:9);
- "great tribulation" (Matthew 24:29);
- "the tribulation of those days" (Matthew 24:29);
- "the great day of his wrath" (Revelation 6:17);
- "the hour of his judgment" (Revelation 14:7).

Several of these verses are followed by statements indicating that this is not the eternal state, that there is yet something to follow:

- "but he shall be saved out of it" (Jeremiah 30:7);
- "even until the consummation" (Daniel 9:27);
- "and at that time thy people shall be delivered" (Daniel 12:1);
- "many shall be purified" (Daniel 12:10);

- "for the elect's sake those days shall be shortened" (Matthew 24:22b).

Jesus Himself describes the timing best of all:

> Immediately after the tribulation of those days shall the sun be darkened, and the moon shall not give her light, and the stars shall fall from heaven, and the powers of the heavens shall be shaken: and then shall appear the sign of the Son of man in heaven: and then shall all the tribes of the earth mourn, and they shall see the Son of man coming in the clouds of heaven with power and great glory. And he shall send his angels with a great sound of a trumpet, and they shall gather together his elect from the four winds, from one end of heaven to the other (Matthew 24:29-31).

In light of passages such as 1 Thessalonians 4:15-18 and 1 Corinthians 15:51, 52, I trust that the bride of Christ may be "caught up" before that dreadful tribulation. "For God hath not appointed us to wrath, but to obtain salvation by our Lord Jesus Christ."[19]

These solemn warnings remind me to respond charitably to those who disagree with me, and I trust my beloved brothers in Christ to bear charitably with me. We stand together in brotherly love, helping each other to beware of sinning willfully.

---

1. See Acts 26:11.
2. Matthew 26:14-16; Luke 22:2-6.
3. Psalm 41:9.
4. Matthew 28:12-15.
5. See Acts 4:6-22.
6. Acts 26:9-11.
7. Acts 23:1.
8. Acts 24:16.
9. 2 Timothy 1:3.
10. John 12:43.
11. Leviticus 10:1, 2.
12. Exodus 19:5; Psalm 135:4.
13. Deuteronomy 32:10; Zechariah 2:7, 8.
14. Amos 3:2.
15. Hebrews 12:6.
16. Hebrews 10:31.
17. Malachi 4:5.
18. Isaiah 2:12; 13:6, 9; Ezekiel 13:5; 30:3; Joel 1:15; 2:1, 2, 11, 31; 3:14; Amos 5:18, 20; Obadiah 15; Zephaniah 1:7, 14; Zechariah 14:1; Malachi 4:5; Acts 2:20; 1 Thessalonians 5:2; and finally 2 Peter 3:10.
19. 1 Thessalonians 5:9.

7

Beware of Drawing Back

Now the just shall live by faith: but if any man draw back, my soul shall have no pleasure in him (Hebrews 10:38).

There is none righteous, no not one: . . . [we] are all gone out of the way, [we] are together become unprofitable; there is none that doeth good, no, not one (Romans 3:10-12).

None of us is capable of attaining righteousness on our own. We can become righteous only as we live by faith in Jesus Christ.

Whom God hath set forth to be a propitiation through faith in his blood, to declare his righteousness for the remission of sins that are past, through the forbearance of God; To declare, I say, at this time his righteousness: that he might be just, and the justifier of him which believeth in Jesus (Romans 3:25, 26).

The "just" means those who are justified (made righteous) by faith in Christ. The Greek word *dikaios* occurs eighty-one times in the New Testament. It is translated "righteous" 41 times, "just" 33 times, "right" 5 times, and "meet" twice. So *righteous* is a Biblical synonym for "just," or for those who live by faith. Salvation cannot be obtained except by faith in Christ.

In Hebrews 10:38 we are confronted again with an "if," which, according to some people, suggests that whatever follows is an impossibility. The German rendering has no "if," but begins a new statement, firmly positive. This statement means to flinch, waver, abandon, slink away from, or, in this case, to abandon the faith that gives life. Of such God says, "My soul shall have no pleasure in him."[1] I see it as a warning for the Christian to beware of giving up, of drawing back, of failing to continue steadfast in the faith.

Drawing back and failing to trust God fully was the failure and undoing of Israel at the very border of the promised land. God had led them safely through the Red Sea on dry ground, and safely "through that great and terrible wilderness, wherein were fiery serpents, and scorpions, and drought, where there was no water."[2] He also had promised to drive out the inhabitants of Canaan, and to give the land to Israel. Moses had said,

> Behold, the LORD thy God hath set the land before thee: go up and possess it, as the LORD God of thy fathers hath said unto thee; fear not, neither be discouraged (Deuteronomy 1:21).

The Israelites had arrived at the border of the promised land. God meant to give them possession of the land by a series of miracles. But ten of the twelve spies shattered the faith of the people, and they drew back from God's plan and purpose.[3] As a result, they had to wander another thirty-eight years in the wilderness, until all their men of war except Caleb and Joshua had died. None of those who drew back ever obtained possession of the land God wanted to give them. They did not trust God to do what He had clearly promised.

We must remember that the Israelites' only claim to this land was merely by the goodness and grace of God. They had never owned it before, and there was no way for them to earn it. Even their father Abraham, to whom the promise was first made, and who had lived in it for nearly one hundred years, had "none inheritance in it, no, not so much as to set his foot on."[4] But as a token of God's infinite grace, the land wherein Abraham sojourned as a stranger was, and still is, promised to his seed after him, for an everlasting possession.[5] Those who drew back at Kadesh-barnea died in the wilderness without obtaining it, but their children did obtain it.

After Joshua died, "there arose another generation after them, which knew not the LORD."[6] Because they drew back, turning away from God, He "sold them into the hands of their enemies round about."[7] Whenever they or their children sincerely repented, He sent them a deliverer. That happened seven times over, as recorded in the Book of Judges. The record describes seven apostasies, always resulting in dire straits for Israel.

In the days of Samuel, at Israel's request, God gave them a king in the person of Saul (ten years before David was born). By 931 B.C., the kingdom was divided. In 722 B.C., the Northern Kingdom was carried into Assyria, and in about 586 B.C., the Southern Kingdom of Judah was deported to Babylon. Jerusalem, along with Solomon's magnificent temple, was destroyed by fire. All of these sad disasters were the results of God's people drawing back from faithfully trusting and serving God.

But God, who always keeps His promises, brought them back again. Jerusalem was rebuilt, the temple was replaced, and Israel was restored, all by the marvelous grace of God. In due time, God made good the first and most amazing promise of all times. He sent Jesus Christ, His co-eternal and co-equal Partner, the One "by whom also he made the worlds,"[8] and by Whom also, at the end of time, He will judge the world in righteousness and truth.

Jesus lived in the midst of the Jews for thirty-three years. He spent at least three years preaching and teaching the Gospel to all the people. But the official religious leaders of that day drew back and rejected Him. They finally demanded, "Away with Him! Crucify Him!"[9] He gave His life on the cross of Calvary, shedding His own blood for the salvation of whoever would place their faith in Him.

After all that, they still refused His teachings and martyred most of His apostles. Their massive rejection of Christ led finally to the second destruction of Jerusalem in A.D. 70, and the dispersion of Israel throughout the whole earth, just as God had forewarned. But God is not finished with Israel. He never was and never will be defeated.

Jesus had come in a way entirely different from what Israel had expected. He who had always been "in the form of God,"[10] the Architect and Creator of the universe,[11] came in the form of a helpless little baby. He grew to manhood in the despised little village of Nazareth, in that half-heathen country of Galilee, out of which they declared "ariseth no prophet."[12] [But Jonah and Nahum had both come from Galilee.]

They expected the Messiah to be the "Wonderful, Counselor, The mighty God, The everlasting [eternal] Father, The Prince of Peace." They had read it in Isaiah 9. Isaiah had even said,

> The government shall be upon his shoulder. . . . Of the increase of his government and peace there shall be no end, upon the throne of David, and upon his kingdom, to order it, and to establish it with judgment and with justice from henceforth even for ever. The zeal of the LORD of hosts will perform this (Isaiah 9:6b, 7).

Their evaluation was exactly right, but their timing was totally wrong! Isaiah did say all of that, and much more. Unfortunately, they had overlooked and totally ignored the first two phrases, which foretold His first coming: "For unto us a child is born, unto us a son is given." They saw only what they were looking for and wanted to see.

The two events foretold in Isaiah 9:6 are separated on paper by only a colon (:), but in time they are separated by more than two thousand years. We might ask ourselves which is worse: to overlook the first, or to overlook the last. Notice that the first is confined to thirteen words, and the last consists of seventy-five words.

Notice also how Jesus respected that two-thousand-years gap in a similar prophetic passage. In Nazareth He went into the synagogue and read from Isaiah. In the middle of Isaiah 61:2, at a comma in midsentence, He stopped reading, closed the book, and started preaching. His theme is recorded in Luke 4:16-20. That passage spans most of the same gap covered by Isaiah 9:6, divided here only by a comma in our Bibles, but divided by two thousand years in time. What He read from Isaiah 61:1, 2, and then preached about, had to do with His ministry in the flesh here on earth. What He did not read, "the day of vengeance of our God," perhaps referring to the great tribulation, and mentioned again in Isaiah 63:1-6, still lies in the future.

The rest of Isaiah 61 and 62 speaks mainly of future things, as do many other passages in Isaiah. Prophetic nuggets abound throughout Isaiah, foretelling the future restoration of Israel.[13] Of the sixteen prophetic books in the Old Testament, only Jonah is totally silent about the future restoration of Israel.

In Nahum 2:2, the King James Version says, "The LORD hath turned away the excellency of Jacob." But eight other translations say, "The LORD will restore the excellence, or the splendor, of Jacob." Luther's German says, "The Lord will bring again the splendor of Jacob."

While we thank God for the scores of prophetic Scriptures already fulfilled in our day, let us beware of unwittingly rejecting scores of futuristic passages scattered from Genesis through the Revelation. Prophecies pertaining to His first and second comings are intermingled throughout the Scriptures. All that pertained to His first coming has been fulfilled to the letter. That should give us assurance that all the prophecies pertaining to His second coming also will be literally fulfilled.

We know of others who draw back from Christ's Sermon on the Mount, saying that it is not intended for our day. Many more draw back from John 13, Romans 12:2, 1 Corinthians 11:1-16, 1 Timothy 2:9-15, and similar passages that denounce the prevailing cultures of the day. But God's Word has stood the test of the ages, and it will stand unchallenged throughout eternity.

Let us not draw back in disbelief just because we cannot fully comprehend it all. The faith by which we obtain salvation trusts the promises of God even when they surpass our capacity to understand. "That in the ages to come he might shew [to us more fully] the exceeding riches of his grace."[14] Only then will we have the capacity to comprehend fully.

Beware of drawing back in unbelief.

---

1. Hebrews 10:38.
2. Deuteronomy 8:15.
3. Numbers 14.
4. Acts 7:5.
5. Genesis 17:8; 48:4.
6. Judges 2:10.
7. Judges 2:14.
8. Hebrews 1:2.
9. John 19:15.
10. Philippians 2:6.
11. John 1:10; Colossians 1:16.
12. John 7:52.
13. For example, Isaiah 1:25-27; 2:4; 4:3, 4; 10:20, 21; 11:10-12; 12:1-6; 14:1-3, 24-27; 19:23-25; 24:23; 25:8, 9; 31:4, 5; 32:1, 2; 35:8-10; 43:1-7; 49:20-23; 51:22, 23; 54:1-17; 62:1-4.
14. Ephesians 2:7.

8

Beware of Not Hearing Jesus Christ

See that ye refuse not him that speaketh. For if they escaped not who refused him that spake on earth, much more shall not we escape, if we turn away from him that speaketh from heaven (Hebrews 12:25).

This reminds us how the children of Israel refused to hear God when He spoke to them on earth from Mount Sinai. When they heard the thunder and the trumpet, and saw the lightning and the mountain smoking, they were gripped with awesome fear. So much so that

They said unto Moses, Speak thou with us, and we will hear: but let not God speak with us, lest we die (Exodus 20:19).

They had committed themselves to do all that the Lord had spoken.[1] But within forty days, while Moses was still on Mount Sinai, they violated their commitment and broke God's commandment by worshiping the golden calf. They not only declined from hearing with their ears, but disregarded what they very well knew in their hearts. Our text suggests it may be even more serious for us to turn away and not hear when God speaks from heaven.

Today, in addition to the Old Testament, we are fortunate to have the New Testament, with a written record of the life and ministry of Jesus. Furthermore, we have much additional information, for in the New Testament God

hath in these last days spoken unto us by his son, whom he hath appointed heir of all things. . . . (Hebrews 1:2).

Because of this, we are more accountable than the scribes and Pharisees were.

The scribes and Pharisees, and many other sophisticated leaders among the Jews, rejected any teaching that threatened their personal preeminence. Luke 4:16-30 records the first sermon that Jesus preached in Nazareth, His home village. He used Isaiah 61:1 and the first clause of verse 2 as His text. It was a most appropriate passage for the occasion, a prophetic revelation of Jesus' ministry in the flesh, which was just beginning. He did not include the second clause of verse 2, which has to do with His Second Coming. His message and the portion He read spoke of things which that day were being fulfilled in their ears.[2]

The people were amazed by His teaching.

> And all bare him witness, and wondered at the gracious words which proceeded out of his mouth. And they said, Is not this Joseph's son? (Luke 4:22).

But in the next five verses Jesus revealed truths that hurt, and they felt threatened. Then they were "filled with wrath, . . . thrust him out of the city," intending to throw Him headlong down over a cliff. Miraculously, He escaped out of their hands, and "passing through the midst of them went his way." No wonder Jesus pleads with us to hear!

I am forcefully reminded how frequently Jesus warned us to hear when He speaks. Eight times the synoptic Gospels quote Jesus' plea, "He that hath ears to hear, let him hear."[3] Eight times in The Revelation, speaking from heaven, He said, "He that hath an ear, let him hear what the Spirit saith unto the churches."[4] It was the heart cry of Jesus that we should beware of not hearing (or not accepting) New Testament revelation. After all, the New Testament substantiates and clarifies what had been prophesied and foreshadowed in the Old Testament.

Jesus illustrated much of His public teaching with parables. His disciples asked, "Why speakest thou unto them [the general public] in parables?"[5]

He answered and said unto them,

Because it is given unto you to know the mysteries of the kingdom of heaven, but to them it is not given (Matthew 13:11).

The word "mystery" (singular) occurs twenty-two times and "mysteries" (plural) five times in the Bible, used only by Jesus and Paul. A mystery is truth

which in other ages was not made known unto the sons of men, as it is now revealed unto his holy apostles and prophets by the Spirit; that the Gentiles should be fellowheirs, and of the same body, and partakers of his promise in Christ by the gospel (Ephesians 3:5, 6).

Because they seeing see not; and hearing they hear not, neither do they understand. And in them is fulfilled the prophecy of Esaias, which saith, By hearing ye shall hear, and shall not understand; and seeing ye shall see, and shall not perceive: For this people's heart is waxed gross, and their ears are dull of hearing, and their eyes they have closed; lest at any time they should see with their eyes and hear with their ears, and should understand with their heart, and should be converted, and I should heal them (Matthew 13:13-15).

Jesus yearned for their conversion, but because they were neither willing to hear nor to be instructed, He dealt with them according to their deceit. Free grace must be received willingly.

The Parable of the Sower
Matthew 13:3-23

The three synoptic Gospels all quote portions of this parable, which is also a parable of the soils. Matthew 13 is the most extensive, and includes more analysis, as well as several other parables. Repeatedly, in verses 9, 13-23, and 43, Jesus warns His audience to be attentive—to hear.

In this parable, Jesus identified neither the sower nor the seed. The sower may be a mother teaching her child at home, a Sunday school teacher, a Christian teacher in the classroom, an evangelist or pastor in the pulpit. The sower could also be anyone passing out Gospel tracts, witnessing on the street, to a next door neighbor, or to a fellow laborer on the job. The emphasis, however, seems not to be on the sower or the seed but the condition of the soil (the heart of the hearer). This determines the yield.

The Parable of the Wheat and the Tares
Matthew 13:24-30

Another parable put he forth unto them, saying, The kingdom of heaven is likened unto a man which sowed good seed in his field: but while men slept, his enemy came and sowed tares among the wheat, and went his way. But when the blade was sprung up, and brought forth fruit, then appeared the tares also. So the servants of the householder came and said unto him, Sir, didst not thou sow good seed in thy field? from whence then hath it tares?

He said unto them, An enemy hath done this. His servants said unto him, Wilt thou then that we go and gather them up? But he said, Nay; lest while ye gather up the tares, ye root up also the wheat with them. Let both grow together until the harvest: and in the time of harvest I will say to the reapers, Gather ye together first the tares, and bind them in bundles to burn them: but gather the wheat into my barn.

In this case a certain Man sowed good seed in His field. But while men (like us) slept, the enemy sowed tares. Jesus identified Himself as the Sower, the field as the world (of teeming humanity), the good seed as the children (people) of the kingdom, the tares as the children (people) of the wicked one, the devil as the enemy, the harvest as the end of the world, and the reapers as the angels.[6] While drowsy Christians sleep away, the devil hastens to the prey.

The Parable of the Mustard Seed
Matthew 13:31, 32

Another parable put he forth unto them, saying, The kingdom of heaven is like to a grain of mustard seed, which a man took, and sowed in his field: which indeed is the least of all seeds: but when it is grown, it is the greatest among herbs, and becometh a tree, so that the birds of the air come and lodge in the branches thereof.

This parable apparently speaks of the same Man and the same field. It seems to picture the phenomenal growth of the early Christian church, springing from seed that Jesus had planted. But later there was an invasion of things that should find no place in God's church. The birds of the air that come and lodge in the branches thereof sound much like the description of Babylon—"a cage of every unclean and hateful bird."[7] I take the latter part as a warning against the apostate church of the endtime sheltering a wide variety of gross immorality. It is happening right in our midst today.

The Parable of the Leaven
Matthew 13:33

Jesus sowed no leaven, but He warns us of that "which a woman took and hid it in three measures of meal, till the whole was leavened." The woman typifies the church,[8] and leaven in the Scriptures usually, if not always, denotes evil. There was a leaven of the religious Pharisees and Sadducees,[9] of Herod,[10] and of malice and wickedness.[11]

> Beware ye of the leaven of the Pharisees, which is hypocrisy. For there is nothing covered that shall not be revealed; neither hid that shall not be known (Luke 12:1b, 2).

Three measures of meal (proper ceremony and conduct) can neither compensate for the damage nor conceal the leaven that a woman took and hid. Hidden leaven in a church is like a cancer in the body. It may be hidden for a while, but is never harmless. State churches have martyred Christians by the thousands. "He that hath ears to hear, let him hear." Beware of hidden leaven in the church!

The Parable of the Hidden Treasure
Matthew 13:44

Again, the kingdom of heaven is like unto treasure hid in a field; the which when a man hath found, he hideth, and for joy thereof goeth and selleth all that he hath, and buyeth that field.

We must let the Scriptures interpret Scripture, or we will miss the point. Christ is not hid in a field. "The field is the world."[12] And "God so loved the world [of human souls] that he gave his only begotten Son"[13] to save whosoever will hear. Christ is the Man who bought that field at a price which no other can match. The Bible also identifies the treasure[14] hidden in the field that Christ has purchased with His own sinless blood. Having bought the field, Jesus became the legal Heir to all the treasure hidden therein.

The Parable of the Pearl of Great Price
Matthew 13:45, 46

Again, the kingdom of heaven is like unto a merchant man, seeking goodly pearls: who, when he had found one

pearl of great price, went and sold all
that he had, and bought it.

I realize some teach that the pearl of great
price is Christ Himself, and that we must sell
all we have and buy Christ. But the Bible says
salvation is a gift that cannot be bought.

> Ho, every one that thirsteth, come ye
> to the waters, and he that hath no
> money; come ye, buy, and eat; yea,
> come, buy wine and milk without
> money and without price (Isaiah 55:1).

The Bible also teaches that Jesus paid the
full price for our redemption with the only
currency that heaven recognizes, His own
sinless blood. We cannot buy Christ by being
good, for "there is none good but one, that is
God."[15] "All our righteousnesses are as filthy
rags; and we all do fade as a leaf, and our
iniquities, like the wind, have taken us
away."[16]

The Bible reveals Christ as the true merchant man. He came to earth in human flesh
for the express purpose of obtaining goodly
pearls. "When He had found one pearl of

great price, He went to Calvary and gave all that He had, yea, even His very life blood, and literally bought "the church of God, which he hath purchased with his own blood." [17]

The Parable of the Net
Matthew 13:47-50

Again, the kingdom of heaven is like unto a net, that was cast into the sea, and gathered of every kind: which, when it was full, they drew to shore, and sat down, and gathered the good into vessels, but cast the bad away. So shall it be at the end of the world: the angels shall come forth, and sever the wicked from among the just, and shall cast them into the furnace of fire: there shall be wailing and gnashing of teeth.

The Gospel net "was cast into the sea [of humanity], and gathered of every kind." It is possible to enter the Gospel net and become a church member without the new birth. But be not deceived, no one gets into heaven without being born again. [18] The angels shall separate the wicked from the just to be punished.

Counterfeits may be smuggled by here on earth, but there will be no smuggling at the judgment bar of God.

The Test of Salt
Luke 14:34, 35

Salt is good: but if the salt have lost his savour, wherewith shall it be seasoned? It is neither fit for the land, nor yet for the dunghill; but men cast it out. He that hath ears to hear, let him hear.

Salt may be heated red hot[19] or dumped in water and still retain its savour. But its value can be destroyed by dilution (compromise) or filthy contamination (corruption). A Christian testimony always suffers when there is spiritual compromise or moral corruption.

The Conclusion

The six solemn warnings given in the book of Hebrews warn us, as they did the Jews in Paul's day, to beware of the six major sins that Israel committed while Moses fasted and prayed on Mount Sinai. Neglect (of their commitment), unbelief, falling away, sinning willfully, turning back, and not hearing God (inattentiveness to Him) all were involved. Not only then, and not only during the next forty years as they journeyed, but for centuries in the promised land, they violated their commitment repeatedly, grieving God intensely. Professing Christians have done the same.

No doubt the Jews' greatest sin was their rejection of the Messiah when He presented Himself bodily in their midst. They had studied the Scriptures, knew He was coming, and for generations had waited, looked, and prayed for His coming. Finally, He came, lived among them, taught in their synagogues, and preached throughout their land. Then they rejected His message, declared Him an imposter, and crucified Him as if He were the vilest of criminals.

The Revelation substaniates and further clarifies many of the mysteries mentioned by Jesus in the Gospels and by Paul in the

Epistles. Five of the seven churches described in Revelation 2 and 3 are warned to repent. Repentance is imperative for every adult, "for all have sinned, and come short of the glory of God."[20] "He that hath an ear, let him hear what the Spirit saith unto the churches."[21] Let us beware of not hearing this all-important mandate of God. Repentance is as essential in shaking off our sinful past as faith is in laying hold on the promises of God.

Was it not to professors of faith that Jesus said, "Except ye repent, ye shall all likewise perish"?[22] Because "there is no man that sinneth not,"[23] we do well to close each day with a penitential prayer for cleansing from any unwitting sin of omission as well as any sin of commission. Having thus committed everything to God, we can then by faith be assured that God will hear the prayers of all who diligently hear Him.

Beware of not hearing Jesus Christ!

1. Exodus 19:8.
2. Luke 4:21.
3. Matthew 11:15; 13:19, 43; Mark 4:9, 23; 7:16; Luke 8:8; 14:35.
4. Revelation 2:7, 11, 17, 29; 3:6, 13, 22; 13:9.
5. Matthew 13:10.
6. Matthew 13:37-39.
7. Revelation 18:2.
8. Ephesians 6:25; Revelation 17:4-9, 18 (an apostate church).
9. Matthew 16:6, 11, 12.
10. Mark 8:15.
11. 1 Corinthians 5:6-8.
12. Matthew 13:38.
13. John 3:16.
14. Exodus 19:5; Deuteronomy 7:6; 14:2; 26:18; 1 Kings 8:53; Psalm 33:12; 135:4.
15. Matthew 19:17.
16. Isaiah 64:6.
17. Acts 20:28.
18. Matthew 22:10-14; John 3:1-8.
19. I have seen salt heated in an iron kettle until it shone red, for quick curing of pork hams.
20. Romans 3:23.
21. Revelation 2:29.
22. Luke 13:3, 5.
23. 1 Kings 8:46.

9

Beware of Satan's Trinity

And I saw three unclean spirits like frogs come out of the mouth of the dragon, and out of the mouth of the beast, and out of the mouth of the false prophet. For they are the spirits of devils, working miracles, which go forth unto the kings of the earth and of the whole world, to gather them to the battle of that great day of God almighty (Revelation 16:13, 14).

This was one of many visions by which God revealed to John what would happen at the end of time. This may be the first time that Satan is pictured as a trinity, but it clearly reveals his sinister tactics, ultimate goal, and final destruction. It concisely describes the union and united mission of the dragon, the beast, and the false prophet. Satan can never duplicate the triune pattern of God's Holy Trinity, but he desperately seeks to imitate it. Our text reveals Satan's trinity as devils working miracles, but they will be defeated in the battle of Armageddon.[1] That's a universal wake-up call to beware of Satan's trinity.

The dragon is commonly known as Satan (so named fifty-five times in the Bible). When Adam yielded to Satan, Satan became "the god of this world."[2] Ever since then he has been blinding "the minds of them which believe not."[2] The Revelation reveals him as the designer of the Satanic trio, and Satan gives his power and great authority to the beast that rises "up out of the sea, having seven heads and ten horns."[3]

The beast "with seven heads and ten horns," appears to be an end-time demonic civil power, evidently the final fulfillment of the "little horn,"[4] the last and major antichrist. Evidently he is Satan's counterpart or substitute for Jesus Christ. By one of his heads being "wounded to death,"[5] "whose deadly wound was healed,"[6] he may try to fake an imitation of Christ's resurrection from the dead.

The false prophet is so named only in Revelation 16:13, 19:20, and 20:10, but he usually is identified with the second beast, "coming out of the earth; and he had two horns like a lamb, and he spake as a dragon."[7] He will do great wonders and deceive "them that dwell on the earth by the means of those miracles which he has power to do."[8] He will at least pretend "to give life unto the image of the [first] beast."[9]

Whether faked or actual, whatever miracles either the beast or the false prophet may perform will be done by the power of Satan. In the days of Job, God permitted Satan to make fire fall from heaven.[10] In "the hour of his judgment,"[11] God may permit Satan to perform miracles such as we have never seen as a final delusion for those who persist in unbelief. It is far better to take His warnings to heart before "the hour of his judgment is come."

Satan's evil tactics and powers are

revealed progressively throughout the Bible, but only in the Revelation is Satan's power described as a trinity whose ulterior purposes and goals are clearly defined. Moreover, the peak of their demonic powers will hardly be fully reached or revealed until "the great tribulation." Those will indeed be dark days as God's judgment is poured out upon a rebellious world. But praise the Lord, at the end of those days their fiendish demonic powers finally will be crushed, as revealed in the references cited earlier.

> And I [John] saw heaven opened, and behold a white horse; and he that sat upon him was called Faithful and True, . . . And the armies which were in heaven followed him upon white horses, . . . And he hath on his vesture and on his thigh a name written. KING OF KINGS AND LORD OF LORDS (Revelation 19:11-16).

Horses were the fastest and most powerful physical means of conveyance in John's day. Therefore, in his vision, we understand them to be symbols of superhuman speed and power.

Do not the riders who follow Christ include the saints who had died earlier, who "shall rise first: . . . [and also those who] shall be caught up together with them to meet the Lord in the air"?[12] "For if we believe that Jesus died and rose again, even so them also which sleep in Jesus will God bring with him,"[13] evidently when He descends "with power and great glory"[14] to destroy the armies at Armageddon.

John further described the battle of Armageddon in Revelation 19:19-21. The Word of God straight from the lips of Jesus is sharper than any two-edged sword. Therefore, He will not need any metal or atomic weapons to smite the thousands, millions, or whatever number Satan's trinity will assemble at Armageddon. He who spoke the universe into existence and holds it all together by the word of His power[15] could wipe them all out with one breath of His mouth. Revelation 19:20 plainly reveals the final disposal of the beast and the false prophet. That is the last we read of them, but God has additional judgments in store for the dragon, which is Satan himself.

The Revelation is a much disputed book. I used to read it with serious reservations, much as unbelievers read the Sermon on the Mount. That sermon was preached to a multitude in need of milk. It also contained some strong meat that they were not yet able to digest. The night before His crucifixion, Jesus said to His twelve Apostles, "I have yet many things to say unto you, but ye cannot bear them now."[16] Pentecost had not yet come. Revelation 20 is part of those many things, conveyed from heaven by Jesus Himself, through John.

Wanting us to know and understand the truth, He kept it very simple, in very familiar words. He expects us to accept by faith what our finite minds cannot fully comprehend.

Study carefully the first four verses of Revelation 20.

> And I saw an angel come down from heaven, having the key of the bottom-

less pit and a great chain in his hand. And he laid hold on the dragon, that old serpent, which is the Devil, and Satan, and bound him a thousand years, And cast him into the bottomless pit, and shut him up, and set a seal upon him, that he should deceive the nations no more, till the thousand years should be fulfilled: and after that he must be loosed a little season. And I saw thrones, and they sat upon them, and judgment was given unto them: and I saw the souls of them that were beheaded for the witness of Jesus, and for the word of God, and which had not worshipped the beast, neither his image, neither had received his mark upon their foreheads, or in their hands; and they lived and reigned with Christ a thousand years (Revelation 20:1-4).

Verses 5 and 6 of Revelation 20 both mention "the first resurrection," from the Greek word *anastasis,* which occurs forty-two times in the New Testament. Some interpret this passage to mean the new birth. Others, because verse 5 distinctly puts a thousand years between the two resurrections, apply it to the bodily resurrection of the redeemed. We are told that "the dead in Christ shall rise first,"[17] and that the lost will not rise until the redeemed will have "lived and reigned with Christ a thousand years."[18] "But the rest of the dead lived not again until the thousand years were finished."[19]

> Blessed and holy is he that hath part in the first resurrection: on such the second death hath no power, but they shall be priests of God and of Christ, and shall reign with him a thousand years (Revelation 20:6).

Because nothing else seems as plain as the Bible itself, I can no longer make figurative the plain, simple wording of Revelation 20. Having tried that too long, I stand rebuked by numerous passages that plainly declare a final restoration of Israel,[20] a Messianic Kingdom with Christ reigning on David's throne,[21] the binding of Satan,[22] and "the restitution of all things."[23]

The phrase "a thousand years" or "the thousand years" appears six times in the first eight verses of this chapter. While I do not understand everything about the thousand years, I have, nevertheless, come to accept what Revelation 20 states so clearly. God has planned, perfectly understands, and will fulfill every detail in full accordance with His promises.

John's inspired vision continues.

And when the thousand years are expired, Satan shall be loosed out of his prison, and shall go out to deceive the nations which are in the four quarters of the earth, Gog and Magog, to gather them together to battle [one more time]: the number of whom is as the sand of the sea. And they went up on the breadth of the earth, and compassed the camp of the saints about, and the beloved city: and fire came down from God out of heaven, and devoured them. And the devil that deceived them was cast into the lake of fire and brimstone, where the beast and the false prophet are, and shall be tormented day and night for ever and ever (Revelation 20:7-10).

This concludes the Biblical revelation and final disposal of Satan in the lake of fire where the dragon, the beast, and the false prophet, along with all the unsaved, will be tormented for ever and ever. Until then, and especially at the end time, we need to beware of Satan's trinity. They are enemies of God and man, but God and His Word remain faithful and true for ever and ever!

---

1. Revelation 16:16; 19:19-21.
2. 2 Corinthians 4:4.
3. Revelation 13:1-4.
4. Daniel 7:8.
5. Revelation 13:3.
6. Revelation 13:12.
7. Revelation 13:11.
8. Revelation 13:13, 14.
9. Revelation 13:15.
10. Job 1:15.
11. Revelation 14:7.
12. 1 Thessalonians 4:13-18.
13. 1 Thessalonians 4:14.
14. Matthew 24:30; 25:31.
15. 2 Peter 3:5-7.
16. Luke 21:27.
17. 1 Thessalonians 4:16.
18. Revelation 20:4b.
19. Revelation 20:5a.

20. Isaiah 14:1, 2; 35:1-10; 51:3, 22, 23; 54:2-10; 60:3, 6, 9-12; Jeremiah 23:5, 6; 24:6, 7; 32:37-41; 33:14-16; 46:28; 50:4, 5; Ezekiel 36:8-11, 24-28; 37:11-18, 20-28; 38:8; Hosea 2:19, 20; 3:5; 14:4-7; Joel 3:1, 2, 17, 20, 21; Amos 9:8-15; Micah 2:12, 13; Zephaniah 3:13-20; Zechariah 8:11-15; Malachi 3:12.

21. 2 Samuel 7:16; Psalm 2:8, 9; Isaiah 2:2-4; 9:7; 11:1-16; 19:21-25; 24:23; 61:3-6; 62:1-7; 65:17-25; Daniel 2:44; 7:9, 13, 14, 27; Obadiah 17, 21; Micah 4:1-8, 13; Zephaniah 3:13-20; Zechariah 3:8-10; 6:12, 13; 14:9, 11, 16-21; Matthew 25:31-34; Mark 13:24-27; 14:62; Luke 1:32, 33; Revelation 2:26-29.

22. 2 Peter 2:4; Jude 6; Revelation 20:1-3.

23. Acts 3:19-21; Romans 8:19-23.

10

Be Aware of God's Holy Trinity

As Creators

> In the beginning God [Elohim] created the heaven and the earth (Genesis 1:1).

We think of God the Father as the First Cause, the Chief Commander, the Master and Controller of the universe. Elohim is definitely a plural noun, which suggests a united plurality working in unison and perfect harmony. Paul speaks of Him as a plurality, but as one God. He wrote,

> To us there is but one God, the Father, of whom are all things, and we in him;

and one Lord Jesus Christ, by whom are all things, and we [mankind] by him (1 Corinthians 8:6).

"The Spirit of God moved upon the face of the waters."[1] ("Moved" is defined by Strong[2] as a primary root: "to brood.") The Holy Spirit played a vital part in the Creation. And the waters did "bring forth abundantly the moving creature that hath life, and fowl that may fly above the earth."[3] The enormous variety and volume of fish and fowl that God created exceed our human comprehension.

We have no record of when or how the multiple millions of angels were created. May we not reasonably assume that the Holy Spirit was actively involved in their creation as well? Because of His personality and function, it seems most reasonable to believe that the Holy Spirit participated in the creation of everything that has breath or spirit, and that He continues to provide for their care.

The Gospel of John points to a beginning in eternity past, aeons of time before the Creation described in Genesis.

> In the beginning was the Word, and the
> Word was with God, and the Word was
> God. The same was in the beginning
> with God (John 1:1, 2).

The first chapter of Genesis also puts special emphasis on the Word. Ten times it declares that "God said." When God spoke the world into existence, He did it by the Word, and that Word was Christ.

The New Testament repeatedly affirms Jesus' creative role.

> All things were made by him; and
> without him was not any thing made
> that was made. . . . He was in the world,
> and the world was made by him, and
> the world knew him not (John 1:3, 10).

> For by him were all things created, that
> are in heaven, and that are in earth,
> visible and invisible, whether they be
> thrones, or dominions, or principalities, or powers: all things were created
> by him, and for him: and he is before
> all things, and by him all things consist
> (Colossians 1:16, 17).

God hath in these last days spoken
unto us by his Son, . . . by whom also
he made the worlds (Hebrews 1:2).

Both Genesis and John reveal plurality,
relationship, and unity. "God said, Let us
make man in our image, after our likeness."[4]
"God is love,"[5] which requires relationship.
Love could not exist without something or
someone to love. Obviously, there actually
was a Holy Trinity of nonphysical Spirits, a
Triunity of Holy Personalities, who eventu-
ally created a physical universe and living
creatures in physical bodies. It took God's
Holy Trinity to give us physical life, and we
need this Holy Trinity daily for constant pres-
ervation.

For Conservation

Our finite minds are not capable of per-
ceiving the perfect and total unity possible
only in the Holy Trinity. Perhaps a network
of computers within a corporation provide
an example we can more nearly understand.
Picture a medical team with offices in three
adjoining townships. The medical records of

all their patients are constantly updated and kept identical on one central computer accessed at all three places of business. Far more accurate and uniform, God's eternal Trinity has always been of one mind. This Trinity consists of three Persons thinking identical thoughts in perfect harmony. They have a perfect unity that cannot be matched.

Our triune God created the universe out of nothing and controls it with a spoken word. He set the sun, moon, stars, and planets in precise orbits so that man's timepieces and calendars are set and regulated by these orbits. He governs animals, fowl, and fish with an inherent instinct. Only men and angels were created with the freedom and responsibility of choice. However, men and some of the angels have violated and transgressed God's laws of order, and all nature suffers as a result. Thorns, thistles, weeds, and destructive animals are the results of fallen angels and fallen man.

"Trinity," "omniscience," "omnipotence," and "sovereign" are words not found in the King James Version. However, the Creation of the universe and God's plan of redemption have so adequately demonstrated those four attributes of God that adding these words could not make the Scriptures more convincing. If you are interested in researching the Trinity further, see chapter one of the author's book *Seeing Christ in the Old Testament*.[6] If you want something more scholarly, see *The Great Doctrines of the Bible* by William Evans. If you want something indisputable and indestructible, study the Bible. Because the Bible is timeless, it anchors our life in eternity. Our temporal needs are for this life only, but our spiritual needs are eternal.

For Redemption

Because God knew all things from eternity past,[7] He knew before creating anything that both angels and men would fall into sin. The Holy Trinity was not taken by surprise when that happened. They had their plans all ready. Apparently, the Second Person of the Godhead had already agreed to empty Himself of the form of God and be made in the likeness of men, to reduce Himself from the role of Creator to that of a bondservant and suffering Savior.[8]

A major difference between men and angels is that angels are not born and do not reproduce.[9] They all were created by God, equipped with instant intellectual maturity. They did not descend from fallen ancestors, but are "all ministering spirits." Angels who fell, as many of them have, did so by their own choice, and we find no indication of any redemption offered for fallen angels.

Of the human race, however, God created only two people, and they both fell. All others are their descendants, and therefore were born with a fallen nature, not by choice, but inherited from fallen ancestors. Not only some of us, but "all have sinned, and come short of the glory of God."[10] Jesus voluntarily came all the way from heaven, went to the cross, and with His own sinless blood paid the full price of our redemption.[11] He suffered more for our redemption than any of us have ever suffered for Him! He offers salvation to all by the cross.

"No man hath seen God [the Father][12] at any time."[13] Therefore, all the theophanies of God in the Old Testament must have been Christophanies (visible appearances of Christ, instead of the Father). He talked with Abraham.[14] I do not know of one case in which God the Father or God the Holy Spirit took on physical form. Jesus, even in the flesh, was still "God with us,"[15] "For in him dwelleth all the fulness of the Godhead bodily."[16]

The Father knew He could trust Jesus; although stripped of the basic prerogatives of Deity in being made flesh, to be "in all points tempted like as we are," He never once fell into sin.[17] And Jesus fully trusted the Father. His dying words on Calvary were, "Father, into thy hands I commend my spirit."[18] He was absolutely sure of His resurrection on the third day.[19]

The Father and the Son had absolute assurance in saying that,

> When He, the Spirit of truth has come,
> He will guide you into all truth; for He
> will not speak on His own authority,

but whatever He hears He will speak;
and He will tell you things to come
(John 16:13, NKJV).

The Father, Son, and Holy Spirit fully understand each other. They are always unanimous in everything that any One of them thinks, says, or does. Nothing can be more reassuring than the inseparability and the absolute unanimity of a Triune Godhead that cannot err and cannot fail.

For Consummation

When the world became too wicked, God destroyed mankind with a universal flood, but spared eight people, with whom He re-populated the earth.[20] When the sins of Sodom and Gomorrah exceeded God's toler-ance, He destroyed the inhabitants with fire. But "God remembered Abraham, and sent Lot out of the midst of the overthrow."[21] Today, this wicked world is again madly rac-ing in a headlong plunge of defiance against God.

The second Psalm, attributed to David,[22] has an important message for the present and the future. It also may have had some local application in David's day, but its basic message is definitely Messianic, revealing some future activities of the Father, Son, and Holy Spirit. It consists of twelve verses that can be divided into four sections of three verses each.

Psalm 2:1-3 says the heathen rage, and kings of the earth set themselves against the only true God and His Anointed—exactly what Islamic nations and thousands of Americans are doing today. They plan and boast of breaking free from God's restrictions, denying the fact that they are answerable to God.

In verses 4-6, the Lord responds in sore displeasure, warning that He has, and will yet, set His king upon the holy hill of Zion, and He will be in control. David's victory over all his enemies only foreshadowed the greater David, of whose "government and peace there shall be no end."[23]

David by divine inspiration wrote, possibly a thousand years before Christ was born, quoting Jesus as saying,

The Lord hath said unto me, Thou art
my Son; this day [the day of His incar-
nation] have I begotten thee (Psalm
2:7).

Verses 8 and 9 are what the Father has
promised to Jesus, speaking of power that
neither David nor any other mortal king has
ever had.

The last three verses seem to be the Holy
Spirit warning the kings of the earth to

Kiss the Son, lest he be angry, and ye
perish from the way, when his wrath
is kindled but a little. Blessed are all
they that put their trust in him (Psalm
2:10-12)

We certainly can, and gladly do, depend
on God's Holy Trinity for all our eternal
needs, even beyond the end of time.

For the Lord himself shall descend
from heaven with a shout, with the
voice of the archangel, and with the
trump of God: and the dead in Christ
shall rise first: Then we which are alive
and remain shall be caught up together

with them in the clouds, to meet the
Lord in the air: and so shall we ever be
with the Lord. Wherefore comfort one
another with these words (1 Thessalonians 4:16-18).

Even so come, Lord Jesus.

1. Genesis 1:2.
2. *The Exhaustive Concordance* by James Strong.
3. Genesis 1:20.
4. Genesis 1:26.
5. 1 John 4:7-10.
6. *Seeing Christ in the Old Testament* may be purchased from Vision Publishers, Inc. See the order form in the back of this book.
7. Job 26:6; 31:4; 34:21; Psalm 147:5; John 2:24; 16:3; 21:17; Acts 1:24; Hebrews 4:13; 1 John 3:20.
8. Philippians 2:6-8.
9. Matthew 22:23-30.
10. Romans 3:23.
11. Romans 3:24; 1 Corinthians 1:30; Galatians 3:13; Philippians 2:6-8; Colossians 1:14; Titus 2:14; Hebrews 9:12; 1 Peter 1:18; Revelation 5:9.
12. John 6:46.
13. John 1:18; 1 John 4:12.
14. Genesis 12:1, 7; 13:14; 15:1-18; 17:1-22; 18:1-3, 13-33.
15. Matthew 1:23.
16. Colossians 2:9.
17. Hebrews 4:15.
18. Luke 23:46.

19. Matthew 16:21; 17:22, 23; 20:19; Mark 9:31; 10:34; Luke 9:22; 13:32; 18:33; 24:7.
20. Genesis 6–9.
21. Genesis 19:29.
22. Acts 4:25.
23. Isaiah 9:7.

You Can Find Our Books at These Stores:

CALIFORNIA
Squaw Valley
Sequoia Christian Books
559/332-2385

GEORGIA
Glennville
Vision Bookstore
912/654-4086
Montezuma
The Family Book Shop
912/472-5166

ILLINOIS
Arthur
Clearview Fabrics and
Books
217/543-9091
Ava
Pineview Books
584 Bollman Road

INDIANA
Goshen
Country Christian Book-
store
574/862-2691
Grabill
Graber's Bookstore
260-627-2882
LaGrange
Pathway Bookstore
2580 North 250 West
Middlebury
Laura's Fabrics
55140 County Road 43

Odon
Dutch Pantry
812/636-7922

Schrock's Kountry Korner
812/636-7842
Shipshewana
E and S Sales
260/768-4736
Wakarusa
Maranatha Christian
Bookstore
574/862-4332

IOWA
Kalona
Friendship Bookstore
2357 540th Street SW

KANSAS
Hutchinson
Gospel Book Store
620/662-2875

KENTUCKY
Harrodsburg
Family Bookstore
859/865-4545
Stephensport
Martin's Bookstore
270/547-4206

LOUISIANA
Belle Chasse
Good News Bookstore
504/394-3087

**Our books may also be found on many
Choice Books Bookracks**

MARYLAND
Grantsville
    Shady Grove Market and
      Fabrics
    301/895-5660
Landover
    Integrity Church Bookstore
    301/322-3311
Silver Spring
    Potomac Adventist
      Bookstore
    301/572-0700
Union Bridge
    Home Ties
    410/775-2511

MICHIGAN
Clare
    Colonville Country Store
    989/386-8686
Fremont
    Helping Hand Home
    231/924-0041
Sears
    Hillview Books and Fabric
    231/734-3394
Snover
    Country View Store
    989/635-3764

MISSOURI
Rutledge
    Zimmerman's Store
    660/883-5766
St. Louis
    The Home School Sampler
    314/835-0863

Seymour
    Byler Supply & Country
      Store
    417/935-4522
Versailles
    Excelsior Bookstore
    573/378-1925

NEW MEXICO
Farmington
    Lamp and Light Publishers
    505/632-3521

NEW YORK
Seneca Falls
    Sauder's Store
    315/568-2673

NORTH DAKOTA
Mylo
    Lighthouse Bookstore
    701/656-3331

OHIO
Berlin
    Gospel Book Store
    330/893-2523
Carbon Hill
    Messiah Bible School
    740/753-3571
Dalton
    Little Country Store
    330/828-2308
Fredricksburg
    Faith-View Books
    4941 Township Road 616
Hopewell
    Four Winds Bookstore
    740/454-7990

**Our books may also be found on many
Choice Books Bookracks**

Mesopotamia
Eli Miller's Leather Shop
440/693-4448

Middlefield
Wayside Merchandise Books
and Gifts
15973 Newcomb Road

Millersburg
Country Furniture &
Bookstore
330/893-4455

Plain City
Deeper Life Bookstore
614/873-1199

Sugarcreek
The Gospel Shop
330/852-4223

Troyer's Bargain Store
2101 County Road 70
Sugarcreek, OH 44681

PENNSYLVANIA
Belleville
Yoder's Gospel Book Store
717/483-6697

Chambersburg
Burkholder Fabrics
717/369-3155

Ephrata
Clay Book Store
717/733-7253

Conestoga Bookstore
717/354-0475

Home Messenger Library &
Bookstore
717/866-7605

Gordonville
Ridgeview Bookstore
717/768-7484

Greencastle
Country Dry Goods
717/593-9661

Guys Mills
Christian Learning
Resource
814/789-4769

Leola
Conestoga Valley Books
Bindery
717/656-8824

Lewisburg
Crossroads Gift and
Bookstore
570/522-0536

McVeytown
Penn Valley Christian
Retreat
717/899-5000

Meadville
Gingerich Books and
Notions
814/425-2835

Millersburg
Brookside Bookstore
717/692-4759

Narvon
Springville Woodworks
856/875-6916

Newville
Rocky View Bookstore
717/776-7987

Springboro
Chupp's Country Cupboard
814/587-3678

**Our books may also be found on many
Choice Books Bookracks**

Stoystown
  Kountry Pantry
  814/629-1588

SOUTH CAROLINA
North Charleston
  World Harvest Ministries
  843/554-7960
Rembert
  Anointed Word Christian
    Bookstore
  803/499-9119

TENNESSEE
Crossville
  Troyer's Country Cupboard
  931/277-5886
Sparta
  Valley View Country Store
  931/738-5465

TEXAS
Kemp
  Heritage Market and
    Bakery
  903/498-3366

VIRGINIA
Dayton
  Books of Merit
  540/879-5013

  Mole Hill Books & More
  540/867-5928

  Rocky Cedars Enterprises
  540/879-9714
Harrisonburg
  Christian Light Publications
  540/434-0768

Stuarts Draft
  The Cheese Shop
  540/337-4224

WEST VIRGINIA
Union
  Yoder's Select Books
  304/772-4153

WISCONSIN
Loyal
  Homesewn Garments
  715/255-8059

CANADA
BRITISH COLUMBIA
Burns Lake
  Wildwood Bibles and Books
  250/698-7451

ONTARIO
Brunner
  Country Cousins
  519/595-4277
Floradale
  Hillcrest Home Baking and
    Dry Goods
  519/669-1381
Millbank
  Lighthouse Books
  519/656-3058
Mount Forest
  Shady Lawn Books
  519/323-2830

**Our books may also be found on many
Choice Books Bookracks**

Order Form

To order, send this completed order form to:
Vision Publishers, Inc.
P.O. Box 190 • Harrisonburg, VA 22803
Fax: 540-432-6530
E-mail: visionpubl@ntelos.net

Name_____

Date_____ Phone_____

Mailing Address _____

City_____State_____Zip_____

God at Work in Saints of Old
   Qty _____ x $6.99 each   = _____
God's Wake-Up Call
   Qty _____ x $6.99 each   = _____
Seeing Christ in the Old Testament
   Qty _____ x $6.99 each   = _____
Seeing Christ in the Tabernacle
   Qty _____ x $6.99 each   = _____

               Total Price _____

Virginia residents add 4.5% sales tax _____

             Grand Total _____

All Prices Include Shipping & Handling
All Payments in US Dollars

☐ Visa   ☐ MasterCard   ☐ Check #_____

CARD #
_|_|_|_|_| _|_|_|_|_| _|_|_|_|_| _|_|_|_|_|

Exp. Date _|_|_|_|_|

Thank you for your order!

For a complete listing of our books, write for our catalog. Bookstore inquiries welcome.